The Aircraft Carrier
VICTORIOUS

The Aircraft Carrier
VICTORIOUS

CONWAY MARITIME PRESS

ROSS WATTON

Frontispiece
Victorious as she appeared in January 1965. *Fleet Photographic Unit*

First published in 1991 by Conway Maritime Press
This edition published in 2004 by Conway Maritime Press
The Chrysalis Building
Bramley Road
London W10 6SP
www.conwaymaritime.com

An imprint of **Chrysalis** Books Group

9 8 7 6 5 4 3 2 1

A CIP catalogue record for this book is available from the British Library.

ISBN 0 85177 996 4

Printed and bound in Singapore

CONTENTS

ACKNOWLEDGEMENTS

Collecting information to produce a book such as this is never a simple task, but I have been fortunate in many areas of my research in finding many people to help me. I take this opportunity to thank everyone I have contacted over the past two years. I wish especially to thank the following people and companies, who provided plans, photographs and information: Guy Robbins at the National Maritime Museum, Anne Bell at the Fleet Air Arm Museum, Brian Patterson of the Portsmouth Dockyard Historical Society, Buzz Hornett and his colleagues at the *Victorious* workshops (HMS *Daedalus*), Dr G Patience of Stone Manganese Marine Ltd, Mr T O Wardle of Clarke Chapman & Co. Ltd, Mr R T Knowles of Stothert & Pitt, Mr R M Owen and Mr Needham of Francis Searchlights, Mr Ward and Mr Bennett of GEC Alsthom Engineering Systems Ltd, Mr W D Stevenson of Brown Brothers and Company Ltd, Fred Willmott of HMS *Culdrose*, Al Ross for his help on the American fittings, and finally Ern Crimp, Alfred W Rogers, H W Page and B Pollard of the HMS *Victorious* 1941 to 1945 Reunion Association.

Prior to the order in 1917 for the first purpose-built aircraft carrier, HMS *Hermes*, the Royal Navy had relied upon a motley collection of mercantile and naval conversions on which to launch (and occasionally land) aircraft. None of these ships embodied all – if any – of the essential elements of a genuine aircraft carrier, but all contributed in some way to the eventual development of such a vessel. During this same period the role of the aircraft at sea was also undergoing a transformation. Originally envisaged as a useful spotting device for relaying the fall of shot from a battleship's main armament, the aircraft was slowly gaining recognition as an effective striking force in its own right.

The Washington Treaty of 1922 did much to stunt the development of new carriers by placing a limitation of 27,000 tons displacement per carrier, within a total tonnage of 135,000 tons for America and Britain and 81,000 tons for Japan. This limitation remained in force until the end of 1936. Each country was also permitted to convert two 33,000-ton capital ships into aircraft carriers. This additional provision suited the Royal Navy, which had a recognised requirement for five carriers and was thus able to convert the large light cruisers *Courageous* and *Glorious* into carriers during the latter half of the 1920s, in a similar fashion to HMS *Furious* (originally converted in 1917 and more extensively reworked between 1921 and 1925). A special clause in the Treaty enabled the USA to convert her two battlecruisers *Lexington* and *Saratoga*, which finally displaced 38,500 tons, under the pretext of permitting modifications to existing capital ships in order to protect them from underwater and air attack.

During the remainder of the 1920s the British Government continued to attempt to reduce the cost of defence spending by the restriction of warship size via treaty. Britain proposed a carrier limitation of 23,000 tons for the 1927 Geneva Conference, and, when this was not accepted, advocated a 25,000-ton limit for the 1929 negotiations. The Washington Treaty had forbidden any new carrier building by Britain for ten years, but by 1931 the Admiralty was making plans for a new ship; because of the continuing treaty negotiations, it was decided that the displacement would be 22,000 tons. Owing to the plight of the British economy, however, the ship – *Ark Royal* – was not ordered until 1935, by which time both America and Japan had commenced carriers of greatly reduced weights (*Yorktown*, 19,000 tons, and *Soryu*, 15,900 tons respectively). At the second London Naval Treaty in 1936, agreement was reached to reduce the carrier limit to 23,000 tons, but by this time Japan, unhappy with the disparity of three carriers to five for each of her rivals imposed on her by the Washington Treaty, had withdrawn from the treaty agreements (she announced her withdrawal in 1934).

HMS *Ark Royal* marked a turning point in British carrier evolution. She was the first large fleet carrier designed as such, and she incorporated many of the features tried and tested in the previous aircraft carriers, as well as some innovative ideas: for the first time, her flight deck was also the main strength deck. She was also equipped with arrester gear, two hydraulic catapults three aircraft lifts, an island superstructure and an AA armament which became standard for subsequent fleet carriers.

The 1936 building programme allowed the construction of a further two carriers, and it was originally envisaged that these would follow the same lines as *Ark Royal*, using the extra 1000 tons permitted by the London Treaty of 1936 to incorporate minor improvements. However, the Third Sea Lord, Rear Admiral Sir Reginald Henderson, decided that the new carriers should be well armoured to protect them against air attack from heavy land-based bombers. They were required to withstand a direct hit from a 500lb bomb and destroyer gunfire of 4.7in calibre.

With the growing menace of Nazi Germany and the unpredictability of Italy and now Japan, this seemed a prudent measure. Such an increase in armour weight could not of course be achieved easily under the current treaty regulations. It was therefore decided that a sacrifice should be made in the number of aircraft carried. *Ark Royal* was designed to embark seventy-two aircraft in her two-storey hangar, though a maximum of about sixty was envisaged in full operating condition. The extra top weight on the new carriers could be reduced by the installation of a single decked hangar, thus halving the number of aircraft accommodated. However, such aircraft as the Swordfish, which could combine torpedo-bomber and reconnaissance duties, would help to alleviate the lack of space for high numbers of aircraft with individual roles.

The new armoured carriers were known as the *Illustrious* class, of which *Victorious* was the second of the first pair. Article 12(b) of the London Naval Treaty of 1936 stated that other signatories should be provided with certain details of new ships four months prior to the laying of the first keel plates. This should include standard displacement and the number of aircraft to be carried. As the armoured carrier was considered by the Royal Navy as virtually a new type of vessel, it was decided to keep details of the armoured deck secret for a year, until the completion of the first two of the class. This subterfuge caused a considerable dilemma in the Admiralty; it was recognised that the change in published details from *Ark Royal* at 22,000 tons and seventy-two aircraft to the *Illustrious* class at 23,000 tons and thirty-six aircraft would instantly signal some important change in the ships themselves, and the Admiralty and the Director of Naval Construction could not decide on the best approach. Either the published number of aircraft could (falsely) follow the precedent of *Ark Royal*, or it could be argued that no definite decision would be made on aircraft numbers until a later stage of building, or that the actual types of aircraft would affect the number to be carried and therefore that only an approximate figure of fifty to sixty could be given. It was eventually decided to calculate the aircraft capacity on the assumption that a large number of small aircraft could be parked on the forward flight deck, thus giving the same total as for *Ark Royal*.

DESIGN AND CONSTRUCTION
Early in January 1936, the Controller of the Navy, Rear Admiral Henderson, an experienced carrier officer who had commanded *Furious* and had been appointed Rear Admiral, Aircraft Carriers in 1931, awarded the challenge of designing the armoured carrier to the Chief Carrier Designer, W A D Forbes. Forbes had been responsible for the design of *Ark Royal* and the Mk 1 arrester gear. The DNC (Director of Naval Construction) Sir Arthur Johns, who would normally have mediated, was seriously ill and in fact did not return to his position; the development of the new type of carrier was therefore conducted via private consultation between the Controller and his designer.

Rear Admiral Henderson saw the need for an armoured carrier as so immediate that he could not afford to wait for Staff Requirements to be prepared, so he proceeded without them. His only prerequisites were that the ship should be able to withstand a direct hit from a 500lb bomb, carry side armour equal to that of a contemporary British cruiser and be fast. No Staff Requirements had previously been established for such a carrier, almost certainly because such a design was considered unfeasible within the current treaty limits of 23,000 tons.

Forbes and his staff were already very busy with drawings for *Ark Royal*, now under construction. By late February, however, Forbes submitted the first design studies to Henderson. In the ensuing months many more schemes were brought forward, covering a variety of options relating to size, armour, speed, type of armament and number of aircraft.

One thing that was well established was the definite requirement for flight deck protection and the concurrent necessity for defence against underwater and surface attack. Standard sub-surface protection would be that of *Ark Royal*, able to resist a 750lb charge. It was also hoped to upgrade the armament from the 4.5in twin dual-purpose guns fitted to *Ark Royal* to the new 5.25in DP guns fitted in the *King George V* battleships. No suitable upper deck mounting had, however, been developed and this armament therefore proved impossible to include.

By late June, a full sketch design was officially put to the Naval Staff, and it received Board approval within one month. The flight deck over the hangar was covered by 3in NC armour, constituting 62 per cent of the total flight deck area; the hangar was boxed by 4.5in C armour at the sides and ends, while the magazine and machinery spaces underneath were shielded by a 4.5in C side belt and a 3in C armour deck astride the hangar, and also enclosed by 2.5in NC transverse bulkheads. The final design scheme was approved by the Board on 21 July 1936, the final designs of *Illustrious* and *Victorious* were shown to the Board on 30 November, and these were approved within two weeks. Staff Requirements did result in an extension to the side belt 28ft forward and 24ft aft, resulting in an increase in displacement of 100 tons, which had to be compensated by a reduction in ammunition. The hangar was also widened from 60ft to 62ft, allowing clearance between three aircraft stowed abreast. The building drawings and specifications were overseen by the newly appointed DNC, Sir Stanley Goodall.

Aerodynamically, the *Illustrious* class had some advantages over *Ark Royal*; they – in particular *Illustrious* – had a longer 'round-down' at the after end of the flight deck. This was not a radically new feature; it had been adopted by all British carriers since 1918 as an effective means of reducing air turbulence over the deck, making landing a little less hazardous. This round-down was eventually sacrificed during World War II, to provide increased deck parking area; *Illustrious* actually gained 120ft. The forward hull shape, arrived at after various wind tunnel tests, also helped alleviate deck turbulence. The island superstructure and funnel had an aerofoil section, similar to that of an aircraft's wing. *Ark Royal* had experienced trouble with funnel gases being sucked down over the flight deck, and this was reduced in the *Illustrious* class by heightening the funnel by 8ft. Unlike *Ark Royal*, the new carriers could be fitted with only one accelerator or hydraulic catapult, on the port side, since two would have caused serious constriction on the smaller flight deck. Only two aircraft lifts were fitted and these were not armoured.

The approximate cost of building was £4,050,000, which broke down to £1,694,000 for the hull, £702,000 for machinery, and £68,000 for auxiliary machinery. *Ark Royal* had cost £1,496,250 for the hull and £566,779 for machinery, and her total cost was £3,750,000. Orders were placed with the lowest tender, Vickers Armstrong, on 13 January 1937, with *Illustrious* to be built at Barrow and *Victorious* at Newcastle-upon-Tyne; delivery was to be in 39 months.

During the early years of the War the US Navy became intrigued by the concept of the armoured aircraft carrier, especially in its apparent ability to survive heavy bombing. American observers were particularly impressed at the survival of *Illustrious* after being hit by five 1000lb bombs and three 500lb bombs on 10 January 1941 off Crete, then two more hits from 1000lb bombs while undergoing repairs at Malta a week later. She eventually arrived at Norfolk Navy Yard in America for repairs from 12 May to 28 November 1941. Likewise, *Formidable* was hit by two 1000lb bombs on 26 May 1941, also off Crete, and arrived at the Norfolk Yard on 26 August for a three-month repair and refit. This afforded the Americans a good opportunity to study these ships, whose armoured flight decks later stood them in good stead when facing the Kamikaze attacks that were inflicting such damage on the US carriers in the Pacific. They were therefore probably instrumental in the design of the three ships of the American *Midway* class commissioned toward the end of 1945. These carriers were furnished with 3.5in armoured flight decks and weighed over 45,000 tons. The first Japanese carrier with an armoured flight deck of 3in plate was commissioned in May 1944, though she was not of armoured box hanger design.

The first keel plates for *Victorious* were laid on 4 May 1937, though as a result of various delays she was not launched until 14 September 1939, six months after *Illustrious* and one month after *Formidable*, one of the second pair of armoured carriers ordered under the 1937 Programme. The launching ceremony was performed by Lady Inskip, wife of Sir Thomas W H Inskip, Defence Minister during the government of Stanley Baldwin and responsible for the Inskip Award which severed the Royal Navy's dependency on the RAF for air support.

Unfortunately, Rear Admiral Henderson died on 2 May 1939 from exhaustion due to overwork, and so never saw the completed armoured carrier which he had done so much to promote.

GENERAL ARRANGEMENT AND HULL STRUCTURE
As noted above, the requirement for armour in the *Illustrious* class meant that only one hangar deck could be installed if the ships were to remain within the limit of 23,000 tons displacement. *Victorious* had five decks below the hangar deck including the hold. Another two decks, known as

TABLE 1: **PARTICULARS OF ILLUSTRIOUS CLASS**

Name	Ordered	Builder	Laid down	Launched	Completed	Fate
1st group						
Illustrious	1936 estimates	Vickers Armstrong (Barrow)	27.4.37	5.4.39	21.4.40	Scrapped Faslane 1956
Victorious		Vickers Armstrong (Walker)	4.5.37	14.9.39	15.5.41	Scrapped Faslane 1969
Formidable	1937 estimates	Harland & Wolff (Belfast)	17.6.37	17.8.39	24.11.40	Scrapped Faslane 1955
2nd group						
Indomitable		Vickers Armstrong (Barrow)	10.11.37	26.3.40	10.10.41	Scrapped Inverkeithing 1953
3rd group						
Implacable	1938 estimates	Fairfield Shipbuilding (Clyde)	21.2.39	10.12.44	28.8.44	Scrapped Inverkeithing 1955
Indefatigable		John Brown (Clyde)	3.11.39	8.12.42	3.5.44	Scrapped Dalmuir & Troon 1957

gallery decks, were worked around the hangar. Internally the ship was divided into watertight sections by transverse bulkheads, and the frames were 4ft apart. The machinery spaces repeated the same layout as *Ark Royal*, though they were further apart, with petrol tank compartments, evaporator machinery and compressor rooms fitted in between. Longitudinal bulkheads ran from frame 46 to frame 121, dividing the magazines and main machinery spaces into three compartments abreast and these main longitudinal protective bulkheads were of 1.5in DI plating. This arrangement provided increased strength and protection.

The main citadel was surrounded by an air space, oil fuel tanks and the watertight compartment of the double bottom, which was a sandwich protection of air-liquid-air, able to resist a 750lb charge. The oil fuel tanks were 15in wider on the port side and contained 400 tons ballast to counterbalance the weight of the island superstructure and armour around the boiler uptakes. These were flooded with water as the fuel was used. Armour around the main citadel stretched from frame 54 to frame 127, though the original design had only allowed for this to run from frames 61 to 121, where it extended from 2ft under the lower deck up to the hangar deck on the port side. The extra lengths forward and aft were as requested in the Staff Requirements, and extended up to the upper deck only. On the starboard side this 4.5in C armour extended up to the flight deck between frames 73 and 88 to provide protection for the boiler uptakes. It was at the level of the hangar deck that it effectively became part of the box armour of the hangar.

The hangar deck had 3in NC armour worked either side of the hangar running out to the top of the side belt; within the hangar the deck was protected by 1in NC armour. The hangar itself was completely boxed by 4.5in C armour, which also enclosed the bomb lifts and the boiler room vents. Both ends of the hangar were fitted with 4.5in C armoured sliding doors, as it was not possible to armour the two aircraft lifts (45ft × 22ft) placed outside the limits of the hangar and its 3in NC armour protected roof, which comprised 62 per cent of the flight deck. Armouring the lifts would have added over 54 tons in weight to each lift. As it was, each lift could carry a load of 6 tons.

The hangar measured 448ft × 62ft × 23ft at its highest point; there were, however, deep beams at the top of the hangar to support the flight deck and these reduced the height to 16ft. It could be divided into three sections by fire curtains.

The flight deck was the strength deck, and the construction of the deck from plates of armour, rather than overlaying a structural deck, was the first time such a practice had been used on such a large scale. *Ark Royal* had been the first carrier to have the flight deck as an integral part of the hull, providing upper strength. The American carriers did not adopt this feature until the design of the attack carrier *United States*, laid down in April 1949 but never completed. Her flight deck was to have provided the lateral strength of the hull and, as on *Victorious*, this would have been 3in armour. In contrast to the British design, however, the main function of this deck in the *United States* was to have been to prevent the hull from bending, rather than protection against air attack.

MODERNISATION

Work began on the modernisation of *Victorious* on 23 October 1950, and was expected to take 3 years to complete. In November 1951, however, this was reassessed to 4½, and the programme was again revised in January 1952, when it was hoped to finish by August 1955. Work did not progress well and by November 1952 the estimated completion date was October 1956. In June 1953 the fitting of an 8¾-degree angled flight deck was approved, along with reboilering and installing Type 984 radar, all of which pushed the expected delivery time well into 1958. In the event, the ship was ready by January 1958.

The purpose of the modernisation was to bring the carrier up to the required state for operating the much faster and heavier jet fighters which were being brought into service by the 1950s. It was obviously thought cheaper to modernise an existing carrier than to build from scratch. The Admiralty instituted a 9-year modernisation plan in 1948. With the start of the Cold War, Russia had become the main threat, but it seemed unlikely that a war would break out before 1957. *Victorious* was chosen as the best candidate from the *Illustrious* class for such a refit, although *Formidable* was originally provisionally selected. *Implacable* and *Indefatigable* were also scheduled for similar modification in 1953–55 and 1954–57 respectively, and *Indomitable* for conversion to a deck landing training ship in 1957. With the new *Eagle* and *Ark Royal* due for completion during the first half of the 1950s, the Royal Navy would be equipped with five fleet carriers by 1957.

This extensive programme was curtailed in 1952, though work progressed on *Victorious*, as it was evident the cost of such a full-scale programme would be too high. The demise of the Royal Navy carrier had begun. By 1966 only four large carriers remained: *Eagle*, *Ark Royal*, *Hermes* and *Victorious*, and there were no plans for new building. *Victorious* was withdrawn from service the next year, despite initial plans to keep her until 1969.

TABLE 2: VICTORIOUS AS COMPLETED

Length overall	748ft 6in
Length waterline	710ft
Length between perpendiculars	673ft
Beam	112ft
Beam waterline	95.9ft
Draught full load	29.3ft
Displacement standard	23,000 tons
Displacement full load	28,619 tons
Flight deck freeboard	43ft 4in
Flight deck length	742ft
Flight deck width	95ft
Hangar size	458ft × 62ft
Shaft horsepower maximum	111,000
Shaft horsepower normal	92,500
Speed deep	30½ knots
Oil fuel	4640 tons
Endurance at 14 knots	12,000nm
Petrol	50,000 gallons
Complement	1286 peacetime; 1750 wartime after refit in October 1943

TABLE 3: VICTORIOUS AFTER MODERNISATION

Length overall	781ft
Length waterline	740ft
Length between perpendiculars	673ft
Beam	145ft 9in
Beam waterline	103ft 4in
Draught full load	31ft
Displacement full load	35,500 tons
Flight deck freeboard	44ft
Flight deck length	775ft
Flight deck width	147ft
Hangar size	372ft × 62ft 6in
Shaft horsepower maximum	111,000
Shaft horsepower normal	92,500
Speed deep	31 knots
Oil fuel	4850 tons
Endurance at 14 knots	6450nm
Petrol	339,000 gallons
Complement	2400

It was intended to bring *Victorious* up to an improved *Ark Royal* standard, capable of operating jets of up to 40,000lb. For this, the flight deck had to be strengthened, especially beyond the 3in armour. To achieve this, extra deep beams were required, but these would waste too much space. The problem was resolved by taking the upper gallery deck across the hangar and introducing 8ft bulkheads. This was the first time such a practice had been carried out in a British carrier.

The process of reconstruction involved the removal of all decks down to the hangar deck, plus side plating and armour. The ship was rebuilt with a lengthened flight deck, and the side and hangar armour was reduced from 4.5in to 2in and 4.5in to 1.5in respectively. Hangar deck armour astride the hangar was reduced from 3in to 2.5in, and armour inside the hangar to 1in NC. A 4ft bulge was added to the hull, port and starboard, for increased stability and to allow width to the hangar deck and the decks above. The 2in NC armour side belt was refitted over the bulges.

The hangar now had a height of 17ft 6in clear and measured 360ft × 63ft; an extension was added in front of the forward aircraft lift, measuring 52ft × 62ft, and this was known as A hangar. The main hangar could be divided in two by a fire curtain, making B and C hangars. Sliding doors were installed at both ends of this hangar. Two new centreline lifts were fitted. The after lift measured 54ft × 34ft, and occupied the same position as the previous lift. The forward lift was situated 36ft aft of its original position in the old carrier, and was 58ft × 40ft. Both lifts were designed to carry loads of over 17 tons at slow speed and 13 tons normal, and the larger forward lift platform itself weighed 50.5 tons. The lifts again were not armoured. The heaviest aircraft was the Buccaneer S.2, weighing just under 13 tons unloaded.

The most obvious alteration to *Victorious* from the port side and above was her angled flight deck. This was fitted to enable the triangular area by the island superstructure to be used as a parking area, without the danger of fast-landing jets crashing into parked aircraft during abortive landings and also to leave the forward part of the axial deck clear to launch aircraft on the catapults. The support for this angled deck was a sponson structure 124ft × 28ft bracketed to the existing structure between frames 51 and 82. The entire angled deck extended from frames 46 to 140, giving a total length of 376ft and an additional flight deck area of nearly 6000sq ft – it is hardly surprising that a dockyard crane had to be removed when the ship was floated out of dry dock on 19 March 1956! The entire flight deck was now 4ft higher than it had been in the ship as designed, and from the centreline it had a camber of 9in in 100ft. The 3in NC armour was refitted.

MACHINERY

Boilers: Six Admiralty pattern three-drum boilers were fitted, two in each boiler room. They provided steam at 400psi and were fitted with superheaters. Steam generated in the boiler passed from the top of the steam drum into the bottom of the superheater header, from where it circulated through the superheater tubes before passing out through the top of the header and on to the turbines. Above the boilers were twelve forced draught turbo fans, two per boiler. These gave a forced draught to the sides and back and into the front air casing, where the closed front burner registers were mounted, reducing the considerable heat radiated from the boiler.

During the 1950s modernisation the boilers were replaced by new boilers of the Foster Wheeler type operating at 440psi. The originals were becoming worn out and were no longer efficient enough to provide the extra steam required for generating electrical power and suppling steam for the two new catapults. The decision to renew the boilers slowed the pace of the modernisation even further, because it involved the removal of the deck plating above, which had only just been refitted.

Turbines: One set of Parsons geared turbines, consisting of a LP (low pressure) and an HP (high pressure) turbine, were situated in each of the three engine rooms. This unorthodox arrangement had been successfully employed in *Ark Royal*, where it provided more speed and manoeuvrability than a two shaft configuration. Output was 111,000shp for a speed of 30 knots, 92,500shp, for 29 knots and, at half power, 55,000shp for 25 knots. Exhaust low pressure steam from the HP turbine was piped to the centre of the LP turbine through the top of the casing. It then passed over the LP turbine blading to exhaust at both ends to a condenser fitted underneath. The two flow reaction LP turbine also contained the astern impulse blading. The HP turbine was of a combined impulse wheel and reaction blading type and received high velocity steam direct from the boilers. The two turbines drove each of the three shafts via single reduction gearing.

The forward end of each engine room contained a main feed tank of 19.18 tons capacity.

Auxiliary machinery: Each of the wing engine rooms contained a 400kW steam turbo-driven generator; four more 400kW turbo generators were situated in their own separate compartments on the main deck. These provided the ship's electrical supply of 2400kW. Following the loss of *Ark Royal* in November 1941, four emergency 60kW diesel generators were also fitted; these were to provide power for salvage and damage control and some of the armament, should normal supplies be interrupted. During the ship's modernisation the electrical capacity was increased to 4200kW, then again to 5000kW shortly after the ship commissioned, supplied by eight steam and four diesel generators.

Steering gear: One central rudder was controlled by a four-ram hydraulic electrically operated unit in the tiller flat on the lower deck. The roof of the tiller flat was of 3in protective armour. Throughout the ship's life much trouble was experienced with the rudder as it suffered from severe corrosion and cracking, necessitating its replacement several times. The three-shaft arrangement resulted in serious problems with vibration in the stern of the ship, and the propellers were changed and modified on numerous occasions.

SUPERSTRUCTURE

The island superstructure on the starboard side of the flight deck consisted of four decks built around the funnel uptakes. They were shaped for minimum wind resistance, as was the screen around the 2pdr pom-pom on the flight deck, forward of the main structure: the total length of the superstructure was 170ft. The wheelhouse was situated forward on A deck, the first level above the flight deck. There was an enclosed compass platform and external navigating position above this on B deck. The admiral's bridge, captain's sea cabin and admiral's viewing platforms port and starboard were above this. The top deck, D deck, was essentially a gunnery control platform, with pom-pom directors and air lookout sights. Two squared-off extension platforms were added at this level over the admiral's viewing platforms, probably during the January refit at Liverpool in 1944. It is most likely they were for additional air lookout positions.

The modernisation resulted in a completely new island structure. It was smaller (only three decks high and only 130ft long), the front was curved, and only towards the after part did it vaguely resemble the old structure with a long curve on the inboard side. A flying control position was included on the port side forward; this was also curved, but in the extended refit of 1962 to 1963 it was enlarged and given a much more angled shape. The compass platform on B deck was fitted with gas-tight doors to provide an air-tight citadel as part of the ship's nuclear, biological and chemical defence.

ACCOMMODATION

Living space was always short, especially during wartime. In October 1943 *Victorious*'s complement was 1750 men; it had previously been 1286, including an admiral and his staff. The extra congestion meant that only limited recreational spaces could be provided for CPOs and POs. These were situated forward on the upper gallery deck along with the crew's recreation space. This area also provided sleeping billets for 158 men, 17 POs and 36 CPOs. An ice cream shop and soda fountain were also located here.

Most of the crew ate and slept in large messes on the main and upper deck forward. Here they had kit lockers, long wooden mess tables and seats, and on the deck-head metal bars were fitted from which to sling hammocks. Wash places with sinks and limited shower facilities were provided aft of the messes on the main deck.

The ship's main heads were forward of the capstan flat on the upper deck. A bakery (with two electric ovens), chapel, dental surgery and laundry were also on this deck. In the after part of the same deck were located the officers' wardrooms, cabins, bathroom and WCs. More officers' cabins were on the after part of the main deck.

Forward of the funnel uptakes on the starboard margin of the lower gallery deck, was the ship's galley, kitchen and vegetable preparing room. The cooked food was distributed by mechanical lift down to a servery on the upper deck; here it was collected by mess cooks and taken to the mess decks, where electric hot cupboards kept the food warm. The wardroom and warrant officers had their own galleys and kitchen on the starboard side of the upper gallery deck; lifts were again used to transfer food down to the pantrys on the upper deck.

The best appointed accommodation was of course reserved for the flag officer (when embarked) and the captain. This area was on the after part of the lower gallery deck and consisted of a sleeping cabin, day cabin, bathroom and dining cabin. Sleeping cabins were also provided in the island superstructure for the admiral and captain, for when the ship was at sea.

With the ship's modernisation, and the introduction over the hangar of the continuous upper gallery deck and the angled flight deck, more space was available for the crew. Many of the senior rates' messes were now on the upper gallery deck and therefore had to be well lagged for insulation against the heat and noise of jet aircraft landing on the flight deck directly above. Likewise, some junior rates' messes were also provided within the overhang of the angled flight deck, and it was decided to install air conditioning units. However, conditions onboard were still far from pleasant and when the ship was stationed off Kuwait in July 1961 to deter a threatened Iraqi invasion, eggs were fried on the flight deck as a publicity stunt – and 75 per cent of the ship's company suffered prickly heat, though there were few cases of heat stroke.

During the 1960s *Victorious* operated with a complement normally in

TABLE 4: GROUND TACKLE

Anchor	Type	Weight	Cable	Notes
Bowers	Byers stockless	160cwt	2¾in forged steel 22 shackles/412½ fathoms	2 carried port and starboard, for anchoring and mooring.
Sheet	Byers stockless	160cwt	as above	1 carried starboard side until March 1944.
Stream	Hall stockless			1 carried stowed on rail above quarterdeck.
Kedge	Admiralty pattern			1 carried stowed starboard midships lower gallery deck until 1950.

excess of 2200 men, an increase of approximately 85 per cent on the original design estimate. Hammocks were replaced by bunks, and food was no longer consumed in the mess decks. A new ship's company galley was built forward on the upper gallery deck, with a large dining hall for the junior rates.

RIG

The original rig consisted of a tripod foremast, an after telescopic RDF aerial mast, two hinged W/T receiving masts forward, six hinged W/T transmitting masts aft, and three aircraft signalling booms on the port side at flightdeck level. The tripod mast was fitted with a cylindrical screen housing the new Type 72DM aircraft homing beacon; unlike its predecessor fitted to *Ark Royal*, this beacon could be fitted with a high frequency direction-finding loop above. At the top of this mast was a Type 79 air warning radar, a transmitting aerial which operated in conjunction with another Type 79 receiving aerial fitted to the telescopic mast at the end of the island superstructure. The hinged W/T transmitting masts arranged three to port and three to starboard on the flight deck abaft the island were not antennae in themselves, but carried an HF antenna wire running fore and aft between them. They were operational in the lowered position. The receiving masts forward of the island operated in a similar fashion.

During her refit in America in January 1943, *Victorious* was fitted with a US-supplied YE homing beacon at the starboard side of the funnel, and the Type 72DM was subsequently removed. A Type 272 surface search radar 'lantern' had also been installed on top of the signal house by this time. The HF/DF loop had been removed from the foremast and an MF/DF aerial frame fitted to the front of the island. Before the carrier left Pearl Harbor in April 1943 her two forward hinged W/T transmitting masts were also removed.

By the end of *Victorious*'s refit at Liverpool in March 1944, the Type 272 lantern had been replaced by a Type 277 surface search and height-finder radar. The foremast was fitted with extra yardarms to carry various TBS (talk between ships) aerials. Above this was a Type 279 air search radar, which was basically the same aerial as the Type 79 but with a more accurate rangefinding capability. On the foremast platform was a US-supplied SG radar antenna with, above this, a Type 252 IFF (identification friend or foe) transponder, and below a 'hayrake' IFF interrogator for the Type 279 aerial. A new mainmast was constructed aft of the funnel with two strut supports angled forward. This was now able to carry a Type 293 target indicator 'cheese' antenna on a platform aft and its associated Type 242 IFF interrogator forward. On the top of the new mast a Type 281B air search radar was fitted, with its Type 243 IFF interrogator above. The starboard hinged W/T receiving mast forward was fitted with a VHF/DF (very high frequency/direction-finding) transmitter unit. Except for the removal of the YE homing beacon during the alteration to a training ship in the latter half of 1947, this outfit remained with the ship until October 1950.

The modernisation which began in that year heralded great improvements to the ship's rig. The old tripod masts were replaced by a single lattice mainmast and, most notably, the first installation of a Type 984 radar. This large aerial weighing over 30 tons was designed for fighter control and was part of a three-dimensional radar system, featuring continuous accurate height-finding. It could provide air warning at 180nm and was good enough at half this range for fighter control operation. *Victorious*

received her 984 in 1956, *Hermes* and *Eagle* in 1959 and 1964 respectively. The system was the best air defence radar in the world, greatly impressing the US Navy. Its integration with a CDS (comprehensive display system – an early computerised system) obviated the need for the Type 960 long range air search, Type 982 high-resolution air search and the Type 983 S-band height-finder radar which had been standard fit to many of the postwar British carriers.

Atop the mainmast sat a URN 3 aerial outfit for the Type 957 Tacan aircraft homing beacon, which replaced the US Navy's YE outfit in the Royal Navy. Below this a Type 293Q target indication radar was fitted. Numerous diagonal yardarms were fitted with various radio communication aerials. On the after part of the island superstructure, in a 'thimble' radome, was a Type 963 carrier-controlled approach radar. Below the Type 984 on the forward part of the bridge a Type 974 navigational radar was installed. An MF/DF coil was again fitted to the front of the bridge and a VHF/DF antenna unit positioned on a hinged mast on the starboard side forward. This last was eventually replaced by a distinctive plate-shaped UHF/DF unit during the February-to-August 1960 refit. Hinged W/T masts were again used along the after part of the flight deck, two each side, and these were supplemented by whip aerials. The port pair of masts was removed in 1963 and replaced by four whip aerials.

ARMAMENT AND FIRE CONTROL ARRANGEMENTS

Main armament: Although the *Illustrious* class was envisaged with 5.25in guns in the early design studies, these were finally abandoned in favour of the Mk III 4.5in to save weight. Sixteen were fitted, in twin Mk II BD (between deck) mountings arranged in pairs on sponsons, just below and at the corner margin of the flight deck. Their principal use was as heavy anti-aircraft armament; they had a maximum elevation of 80 degrees and were able to fire across the flight deck. Power was provided by a 46hp motor and hydraulic pump.

The high positioning of the mounts presented some difficulties in the supply of ammunition from the magazines on the platform deck. Vertical hoists were used to lift the shells to horizontal conveyors on the upper deck, which led to more vertical hoists supplying the gun bays on the upper gallery deck. These hoists and conveyors were electrically powered and of an endless-chain design. On each side of the mounting to the rear was a revolving scuttle holding three rounds, and the rounds were passed manually from the scuttles to the right or left fuse-setting machines, and then brought to the loading tray. Loading was possible at any angle of gun elevation. The two gun cradles were bolted together, with run-out powered by compressed air.

Each pair of turrets had its own Mk IV HADT (high angle director control tower). Three were at flight deck level and the fourth on top of the signal house. Except for the after port director these were all fitted with Type 285 RDF by early 1943; the HADT on the bridge had been fitted from the beginning. This director was repositioned on the flight deck in early 1944, when the forward pom-pom was removed from the starboard side.

Secondary AA armament: Six eight-barrelled 2pdr Mk VIA★ mountings were provided for close-range AA protection, two on the port side in separate sponsons at upper gallery deck level, two on the flight deck forward of the bridge on the starboard side, one aft of the island on the flight deck and the last on the after part of the island on B deck. During the war, possibly early in 1944, these were fitted with remote power control and water cooling.

Mk III directors were fitted for the pom-poms, with five about the island structure and one in a sponson at frame 62 on the port side of the upper gallery deck. Except for the last, they were all fitted with Type 282 radar shortly after commissioning. During March 1943 these were all removed to make way for six single Oerlikons. By March 1944 four had been reinstated: one forward on D deck, one to starboard of the new mainmast on C deck, one between the island and forward pom-pom on the flight deck and one in the port sponson.

SUMMARY OF CLOSE-RANGE AA ARMAMENT FITTED DURING WORLD WAR II

The first additions to the close-range AA armament came during 1942, when three single Oerlikons were located around the island structure as follows: one on the flight deck behind the forward pom-pom, one on A deck below the bridge and the third on a new sponson on the funnel port side aft at D deck level.

In January 1943, while the ship was undergoing a refit at Norfolk Naval Yard, USA, further single Oerlikons were added, as follows: five in a sponson on the starboard side of the island at B deck, eight on a stern gun platform at upper gallery deck level, one in a sponson ahead of the after starboard HADT, with another aft, one similarly arranged in front of the port after HADT, two in a sponson abreast the port boiler room vents, one ahead of the port forward HADT, one in front of the forward port pom-pom, and two more located one either side of the funnel at D deck level.

From 9 March to 8 April 1943, while *Victorious* was at Pearl Harbor, two quadruple 40mm Bofors Mk 2 mounts were installed, with two Mk 51 directors, on the lower gallery deck forward of the crane, one each side. Two twin 40mm Bofors Mk 3 mountings replaced the after 44in searchlights, and their Mk 51 directors were located in sponsons just aft. The searchlights were relocated in place of two Oerlikons on the stern gun platform. All six pom-pom directors were removed and replaced by single Oerlikons, the two forward 44in searchlights were replaced by single Oerlikons and ten more single Oerlikons were placed on a sponson outboard of the island structure at flight deck level.

By the end of March 1944 the ship had undergone two refits at Liverpool, in which four twin Oerlikons replaced the five singles at B deck level on the starboard side of the island, four replaced an equal number of single Oerlikons on the stern gun platform, the first and last single Oerlikons on the flight deck outboard island were replaced by twin mounts, as were those either side the funnel, and two twin Oerlikons replaced the single mount at A deck. The single Oerlikon forward of the island was removed with the pom-pom. The removal of the telescopic RDF mast allowed the placement of a further twin Oerlikon and the removal of the single on B deck. Twin mounts also replaced the four singles on the port side amidships, while another four were replaced by the reinstated pom-pom directors. The single mounts forward and aft of the rear starboard HADT were also changed to twin Oerlikons.

In early 1945, two single Boffin guns replaced the twin Oerlikons on A deck and single 40mm Bofors Mk 3 mounts were installed in place of the two forward singles in the searchlight sponsons and the outboard twin Oerlikons and 44in searchlights on the stern gun platform.

TABLE 5: **PARTICULARS OF GUNS**

4.5in Mk III

Calibre	4.5in
Length of bore	200.25in
Length of gun	211.75in
Weight of gun including breech mechanism	2.814 tons
Length of rifling	170.92in
Twist of rifling	Uniform 1 in 25 calibres
Weight of shell	55lb
Weight of charge	Cordite SC 11.035lb
Muzzle velocity	2449f/s
Working pressure	20.5 tons/in²
Maximum range	20,750yd/45°
Ceiling	41,000ft/80°
Mounting	Mk II BD (between decks)

3in/50 calibre Mk 22

Bore	3in
Length barrel and bore	150.25in
Length overall	190.02in
Length of rifling	126.13in
Twist of rifling	1 in 32 calibres
Weight of shell	13lb
Weight of charge	3.7lb NC 033
Muzzle velocity	2700f/s
Working pressure	17 tons/in²
Maximum range	13,590yd/43°02′
Ceiling	29,800ft/85°
Mounting	Mk 33

40mm QF Bofors

	Mk I, Mk 2	Mk IX
Bore	1.575in/40mm	—
Length of bore	88.583in	88.578in
Length of gun	148.8in	145.3–145.5in
Weight of barrel	202lb	227–230lb
Length of rifling	75.85in	—
Twist of rifling	1 in 45 to 1 in 30 calibres	—
Weight of shell	1.985lb	1.971lb
Weight of charge	0.694lb NC 025	0.791lb
Muzzle velocity	2890f/s	—
Working pressure	19.5 tons/in²	19.68 tons/in²
Maximum range	11,000yd/42°	10,075yd
Ceiling	22,800ft/90°	23,500ft/90°
Mountings	Mk 1, Mk 2, Mk 3	Mk VI

2pdr QF Mk VIII

Calibre	1.575in/40mm
Length of bore	62in
Length of gun	102.6in
Weight of barrel	125lb
Length of rifling	54,84in
Twist of rifling	1 turn in 30 calibres
Weight of shell	1.684lb
Weight of charge	0.2793lb
Muzzle velocity	2400f/s
Working pressure	16.5 tons/in²
Maximum range	6800yd
Ceiling	1300ft/80°
Mounting	Mk VIA

ARMAMENT AND FIRE CONTROL AFTER MODERNISATION

Main AA armament: Six American 3in/50cal Mk 33 twin mountings were installed on the upper gallery deck, three to port and three to starboard. This was the first and only fit of this weapon in a Royal Navy warship. The original hope was to mount the larger 3in/70cal Mk 6 turret, as later fitted in the three cruisers of the *Tiger* class, but they were not available in time for *Victorious*. The British version of the Mk 33 had the same carriage as the US version, but was provided with an enclosed shield. The elevating gear was an arrangement of separate elevating pinion and arc mechanisms for the two guns, connected by a cross shaft and simultaneously driven by one power drive. A conventional base ring training track was bolted to the deck, enabling a meshing pinion and train power drive to turn the mounting within adjustable stops. Elevating and training drives were electrically powered. The guns were 64in apart, could be loaded and fired throughout a training arc of 100 degrees, and were water cooled. A paraboloidal reflector antenna mount Mk 34 was bolted to the slide of the left gun. This directed the radar beam and received reflected signals from the target.

The fire control system was the Mk 63 and a controlling director was located close to each mounting.

Secondary AA armament: A 40mm six-barrelled Mk VI mounting was provided on the starboard side of the upper gallery deck at frame 120. The original intention was to fit four, and there was even an interim notion to place six while awaiting the 3in/70cal (these could then be removed and supplanted with the latter). However, the multiple Bofors was ultimately very short lived and by the end of the 1960 refit had been removed, along with the associated CRBF (close range blind fire) director.

AIRCRAFT ARRANGEMENTS

Aircraft and bomb lifts: The original concept for the *Illustrious* class had envisaged thirty-six aircraft, half the number of the previous carrier, *Ark Royal*, but considered justifiable if the ship was to be armoured. Two centreline aircraft lifts, located at the outer ends of the hangar, could make the double journey, including the removal of the aircraft, in 30 seconds. Two centreline lower bomb lifts brought ordnance from magazines in the hold or lower deck to the upper deck; a transverse horizontal conveyor by the forward lift transported the load to a lift on the starboard side, and it then continued its journey outboard of the hangar to the flight deck. In a similar fashion the after lift was connected to a torpedo and bomb lift on the port side by overhead rails; ammunition again went to the flight deck.

During the early stages of redesign it had been hoped to install deck edge lifts, as in US carriers like the *Essex* or *Midway* class, and there was even some thought given to providing a stern lift. In the event it proved impossible to have either; one major reason was apparently the low freeboard of the class.

After modernisation, *Victorious* was intended to be capable of operating a proposed complement of fifty-five aircraft. As noted above, the aircraft lifts were greatly improved, with the forward lift being moved further aft. The bomb lifts were also upgraded; the after lift was relocated 92ft aft of its original position and to starboard of the centreline. It was now connected to the upper outboard lift by a bomb lift platform (from about 1963 these were reclassified as weapons lifts). The forward lift occupied much the same position as had the original, but the lower lift was slightly further to port.

Aviation fuel tanks and supply system: Twenty large cylindrical tanks located on the hold deck, in eight separate compartments, contained 50,598 gallons of aircraft fuel. Two of the compartments were between the boiler and engine rooms and three more were forward of the boiler rooms, which meant that 44,180 gallons were stored within the armoured citadel. Aircraft consumed – on average – 30 gallons of fuel an hour by the middle

1930s, but as engine size and power increased so did fuel consumption. *Victorious* would have required 27 per cent more fuel to meet a 1938 theoretical capacity of sufficient fuel to fly her aircraft for one month (flying time was calculated as 60 hours for a TSR and 45 for a fighter).

By June 1950 fuel requirements for the modernised carrier had risen to 279,000 gallons of Avcat, and 60,000 gallons of Avgas. Avtag (gasoline) and Avtur (kerosene) had been dropped in favour of Avgas (high octane gasoline) which was highly volatile and used for piston-engined aircraft and helicopters, and Avcat (diesel fuel) for turbo-prop and jet engines. The explosive nature of Avgas meant that it had to be stored in special tanks, comprising an inner and outer envelope in a ventilated coffer-dam air space. The outer envelope or saddle tank was open to the sea; as fuel was used from a draw-off tank at the top of the inner main tank, sea water entered the inner tank under the fuel. This process eliminated the dangerous vapour that would develop in a half full tank. To ensure that the fuel remained water-free, it passed through float valves which, because of the difference in the specific gravity of the two liquids, cut off whenever water was present. After an aircraft has been fuelled, the Avgas in the piping system returned to the tanks by gravity, and the pipes were cleared fully by a drain and air suction pump functioning through a vacuum tank. A separate system was installed in the ship to de-fuel aircraft, again using the combined drain and air suction pump.

Avcat was not as dangerous as Avgas but was treated with almost equal respect. Both fuels passed through special filtration units to remove particles of dirt and water. Fram filters fitted to the fuel risers delivering to the ring main were used for bulk filtration. Final filtration was by absorbent paper in units connecting to the hoses.

Catapults: The single BH III (British hydro-pneumatic) catapult installed in *Victorious* was able to launch an 11,000lb aircraft at 66 knots. Early versions of the catapult were known as accelerators, and the device had been conceived by W A D Forbes in 1931. It was an excellent method of launching loaded aircraft over the shortest possible distance, and the carrier was freed from the need to turn into wind to increase air speed over the deck when launching aircraft.

The catapults or accelerators were powered by the ship's hydraulic system, which charged eight air vessels located in the turbo-hydraulic pump room on the hold deck forward. When a valve was opened via a relay system from a control position near the flight deck, hydraulic fluid was exhausted from one end of a power cylinder into an exhaust tank. The compressed air from the air vessels then entered the opposite end of the power cylinder (situated in the hangar at upper gallery deck level under the accelerator) and pushed against a piston, connected by rods to a moving crosshead. Each crosshead was fitted with eight pulleys, joined to other pulleys bolted on the ship's structure by wire reeves. This arrangement afforded an eight-to-one velocity increase at the launching trolley, which ran in a single trackway 3¼in proud of the flight deck surface. Hold-back gear applied a measured load, up to a maximum of 10,000lb, to the towing bridle and kept the aircraft in position against the airscrew pull.

The launching trolley was returned to the launching position after the launch by reversing the process and pumping the hydraulic fluid back into the cylinder.

During her modernisation, *Victorious* was fitted with two steam BS 4 (British slotted cylinder) catapults, which had a stroke of 145ft and were capable of launching aircraft of 40,000lb maximum weight at a speed of

105kts. The basic principle was that of two pistons operating in two long cylinders under the catapult track. The pistons were fixed to a shuttle which was hooked to the aircraft by a wire towing bridle. Steam provided by the ship's boilers acted directly on the pistons, forcing them through the cylinders. A holdback bar was used to keep the aircraft in position while her engines were run up to full power, and the combined force of the aircraft's engine and the pressurised steam on the power cylinders broke a calibrated breaking link in the 'holdback', allowing the aircraft to move forward. A steel sealing strip ran the length of the cylinder preventing the escape of steam from the slot on the cylinder, yet allowing the piston and shuttle to move. The forward end of each piston had a retarding ram towards the end of the travel which entered a hydraulic cylinder to slow the forward motion.

The pistons and shuttle were returned to the start position by a small hydraulic jigger operating a grab by wire reevings. This procedure operated on the same principle as the hydro-pneumatic catapult.

Two jet blast deflectors were located behind the catapults for use when the jets ran up to take-off power prior to launch.

A retractable control position was situated between the two catapults, from which loading of the aircraft on the catapult and launching was controlled. Aircraft were positioned for launch by Catapult Ancillary Loading Equipment (CALE), which consisted of two sets of rollers flush with the deck surface. The inner rollers, preset to match the wheel gauge of the aircraft, ran freely, while the outer rollers rotated inward, driven by an electric motor. This meant that no matter which side the aircraft approached the loading position it would be moved until it reached the free-moving rollers.

Arrester gear: Six Mk 4 arrester wires were originally fitted between the after aircraft lift and the island superstructure. These could stop a 20,000lb aircraft, with a pull-out of 150ft. They allowed the forward end of the flight deck to be used as an aircraft park. A further wire was fitted early in 1943, behind the after lift, when the round-down was removed and the American deck landing procedure was adopted. Only four arrester units, placed under the flight deck, were provided to operate the six deck spans, which were held 3in to 6in above the deck by hydraulically operated bow-shaped steel rods. The arrester units functioned when the aircraft hook engaged a deck wire, pulling a moving crosshead toward a fixed crosshead by means of sheaves and reeving. Between the two crossheads was a hydraulic cylinder, containing a ram and piston connected to the moving crosshead, which displaced liquid within the cylinder, thus slowing the aircraft. The displaced fluid passed to air-loaded accumulators through a non-return valve, which was bypassed when the unit was reset. A spline valve controlled the rate of hydraulic fluid flowing from the cylinder, producing a constant pull-out for even deceleration. At one end a control gear gave different settings for particular aircraft.

Four Mk 13 jet arrester wires were fitted across the line of the angled deck, with an equal number of arresting units below, during the modernisation. These could stop a 30,000lb aircraft travelling at 105 knots.

Crash barriers: Two Mk 4 'safety' barriers (though not particularly safe for the pilot) were placed by the after section of the island structure. Their purpose was to stop rogue aircraft colliding with those in the deck park area forward and they operated on a similar principle, though more vigorously applied, to that of the arrester gear. The wire barrier, raised to head height by two support brackets either side, was able to stop a 20,000lb aircraft at 40 knots in a pull-out of 62ft.

A less hazardous barrier, the Mk 6, was fitted during the modernisation; this stopped aircraft by means of vertical nylon straps hoisted between two masts raised by hydraulic jacks. Undrawn nylon packs connected to the bottom edge of the net were pulled out in sequence to slow the aircraft, and most were designed to break at a certain point, thus preventing the aircraft from being catapulted backward. An aircraft approaching at 80 knots could be stopped in 40ft and the nature and arrangement of the net minimised damage to the aircraft.

Deck landing aids: A DLCO (deck landing control officer) was employed on the port side of the flight deck aft to guide approaching aircraft in by a series of hand signals made with small bats. From about January 1943 a special platform was positioned at the side of the flight deck for the DLCO's use. It was provided with a wind screen of individual slats which could be raised or lowered, and it made the batsman easier to see. At this time the FAA also adopted the American system of orders, which were the complete reverse of the British system; for example, the bats held aloft previously indicated that the aircraft should be higher, whereas under the US system the same signal meant that the pilot was too high. The new method proved quicker and reduced the number of accidents, which was of some relief as the current Tarpons and Martlets were harder to land than the earlier Albacores of Fulmars had been.

The speed of a jet fighter approaching the flight deck made all hope of relaying signals of height and speed by hand impossible. The pilot therefore had to control his own landing, and to this end a new system was introduced – the DLMS (deck landing mirror sight). On *Victorious* this was mounted on a special platform on the port side of the flight deck, much further forward than the original batsman's position. A group of four source lights some 168ft aft of the sight shone into the gyro-stabilised mirror and were reflected to the pilot. Either side of the mirror, datum lights of red and green indicated if the pilot was too high or low, or left or right of track, while an audio signal received by the pilot revealed the speed. Another DLMS was situated on the starboard side of the flight deck. In 1963 the mirror sight on *Victorious* was replaced by a deck landing projector sight, which no longer required a separate light source, though it operated on much the same principle.

OPERATION TUNGSTEN

At the beginning of April 1944 the German battleship *Tirpitz*, sister-ship of the ill-fated *Bismarck*, lay at anchor at the top of Alten Fjord, undergoing final repairs to damage inflicted in a crippling attack by Royal Navy X-craft midget submarines on 22 September 1943. Intelligence sources reported that she would shortly be fit to sail.

The Royal Navy was determined to destroy Germany's last capital ship, and the FAA had spent the previous weeks practising bombing runs at Loch Eribol on the north coast of Scotland. Final rehearsals were conducted at Scapa Flow on 28 March 1944 by torpedo-bomber-reconnaissance aircraft from *Victorious* and *Furious*.

The vertical mountain sides 3000ft high along the fjord provided perfect protection for the *Tirpitz*, as she lay inside anti-submarine nets in a stretch of water only ¾ mile wide. This natural protection was supplemented by AA batteries, radar and smoke generators to shroud the ship if she was attacked from the air.

The strike force's passage to Norway was covered by escorting convoy JW58 of forty-nine ships. Force 1, under Admiral Sir Bruce Fraser and

TABLE 6: **PARTICULARS OF SHIP'S BOATS**

Motor boats	Construction	Beam (excluding rubbers)	Speed (knots)	Bhp	Weight	Lifesaving capacity	Notes
26ft motor pinnace	Clinker-built round bilge	9ft 9in	7½	20	130cwt	76	2 carried during war; 2 carried after 1958. Used for liberty men and laying stream anchor.
35ft fast seaplane tender							
35ft fast motor boat	Carvel-built hard chine	8ft 6in	17–22	65/100 twin	90cwt	46	1 carried during war – admiral's barge not carried after 1950.
35ft medium speed boat	Carvel-built round bilge	9ft 2in	12–13	72/144 twin	127cwt	30	up to 3 carried from 1958 – one as admiral's barge.
32ft motor cutter	Clinker	8ft 6½in	7½	43	95cwt	31	2 carried during war; not carried after 1950
27ft motor whaler	Fibreglass round bilge	7ft	6½	11½	18cwt	12	3 carried from 1958. Port boat bay plated over during extended refit in 1965, then only 2 were carried on starboard side.
25ft fast motor boat	Sheer strake clinker-built hard chine carvel-built	6ft 9in	17–23	65/100	45cwt	30	1 carried port side (not carried after 1950).
16ft fast motor dinghy	Sheer strake clinker hard chine carvel	5ft 6in	14–24	24/28	18cwt	12	1 carried port side (not after 1950).
Gemini craft	Rubber inflatable	6ft 10in	18	40/80 outboard	400lb	10	At least 1 carried port side upper gallery deck after 1965.

Sailing boats	Construction	Beam (excluding rubbers)	Rig	Oars	Weight	Lifesaving capacity	Notes
32ft life cutter	Clinker (drop keel)	8ft 6½in	Single mast dehorsey or	8 × 15ft 4 × 14ft	52cwt	59	2 carried during war (not carried after 1950).
27ft whaler	Clinker (drop keel)	6ft	Two mast Montagu	4 × 17ft 1 × 16ft	26cwt	27	2 carried during war (not carried after 1950).
14ft dinghy	Clinker (drop keel)	5ft 4¾in	Single mast gunter	4 × 8ft	10cwt	6	2 carried between stern walkways under overhang of flight deck after 1958. 2 originally carried above 03 deck (not after 1958).

consisting of *Victorious*, *Duke of York*, *Anson*, *Belfast* and six destroyers, sailed from Scapa on 30 March to rendezvous 220 miles northwest of Alten Fjord with Force 2, which comprised *Furious* and the escort carriers *Emperor*, *Searcher*, *Pursuer* and *Fencer*, plus three cruisers and ten destroyers, under Rear Admiral Bisset. On the afternoon of 2 April the attacking force of carriers approached their designated flying-off positions. The first strike, of twenty-one Barracuda aircraft from *Victorious* and *Furious*, escorted by forty-five Corsairs, Hellcats and Wildcats flying CAP (combat air patrol) cover, closed their target on the 3rd.

Unaware of the approaching attack, Captain Hans Meyer was preparing the *Tirpitz* for sea when, at 0528hrs, the alarms sounded on board. The strike aircraft had climbed to 10,000ft some 25 miles from the Norwegian coast, and commenced their dive at 8000ft, releasing their bombs between 3000ft and 1200ft.

Hits were scored on the bridge and amidships, and the strike was over within 60 seconds. The second strike followed the same approach, though the German smoke generators were now operational and beginning to obscure the target. A total of fourteen hits was made, but the two hits by 1600lb AP bombs were ineffective because the bombs had been dropped too low to penetrate the battleship's armour.

The first strike, landed back on board at 0630hrs, the second strike returning at 0758hrs. Three Barracudas were lost.

Victorious arrived back at Scapa on 6 April to a triumphant welcome. Although the *Tirpitz* had not been destroyed, the damage inflicted by Operation Tungsten took another three months to repair. Unfortunately, despite further strikes throughout the summer months of 1944, the FAA was unable to put the battleship out of action altogether.

CAREER SUMMARY

29 March 1941: Commissioned under command of Captain Henry C Bovell.

16 April 1941: Sea trials and maiden voyage to Rosyth.

15 May 1941: Leaves Rosyth for Scapa Flow.

20 May 1941: Admiral Tovey addresses ship's company, telling them of the breakout of *Bismarck* and *Prinz Eugen* into the North Atlantic.

22 May 1941: Sails with the battleship *King George V*, four cruisers and seven destroyers in search of *Bismarck*.

23 May 1941: *Bismarck* sighted by cruisers *Norfolk* and *Suffolk* in Denmark Strait.

24 May 1941: *Hood* and *Prince of Wales* close *Bismarck*; *Hood* fires on *Prinz*

Eugen at 0600hrs, but is hit by salvoes from both ships and sunk. *Prince of Wales* scores a hit on *Bismarck*, but breaks off engagement. *Victorious* and the 2nd Cruiser Squadron detached at 1600hrs to within 100 miles of the enemy, and nine Swordfish aircraft under the command of Lt Cdr(A) E Esmonde are launched at 2214hrs. Forty minutes later three Fulmars of 800 squadron take off for shadowing duties. The nine Swordfish of 825 Squadron are fitted with ASV (air to surface) radar and pick up *Bismarck* 16 miles ahead of *Norfolk* and *Suffolk* at 2327hrs. *Bismarck* spots the approaching aircraft and sends up a heavy AA barrage. Eight Swordfish press home their attack from every quarter, launching torpedoes low over the water; only one hits *Bismarck*, amidships. All aircraft return to *Victorious* safely by 0200hrs.

25–26 May 1941: *Victorious* continues flying off her Swordfish. *Bismarck* is eventually relocated at 1030hrs on 26 May by a land-based Catalina aircraft of 209 Squadron, 690 miles WNW of Brest. *Ark Royal*, approaching from the south, dispatches her aircraft to shadow *Bismarck* at 1115hrs.

9–11 June 1941: *Victorious* transfers 24 Hurricanes to *Ark Royal* at Gibraltar.

13 June 1941: Departs with *Ark Royal*, *Renown* and seven destroyers for Malta.

23 July 1941: Sails from Scapa Flow as part of Force P in company with *Furious*, *Suffolk*, *Devonshire* and six destroyers to attack enemy transports in Norway and Finland.

30 July 1941: Arrives 80 miles northeast Kirkenes, northern Norway. Carriers launch their aircraft at 1400hrs. Unfortunately, the ships are spotted by a German reconnaissance aircraft, so AA batteries are prepared and German fighters are scrambled to attack the incoming aircraft; eleven Albacores and two Fulmars are lost.

23 August 1941: Sails in company with *Devonshire*, *Suffolk* and three destroyers (as Force M) from Scapa Flow, to rendezvous with *Argus*.

3 September 1941: Carries out air attacks against shipping and oil storage tanks at Hammerfest, Norway.

12 September 1941: Air strikes against shipping and aluminium works at Glomfjord and D/F station at Rost Island, Norway.

13 September 1941: Back at Scapa Flow.

19 February 1942: Sails with battleship *King George V*, cruiser *Berwick* and seven destroyers for Tromso.

21 February 1942: Alters course south to intercept German warships *Admiral Scheer* and *Prinz Eugen*.

22 February 1942: Albacores flown off to search for the two enemy ships; bad weather conditions prevent any detection.

9 March 1942: Launches six Albacores to search for *Tirpitz*, then twelve Albacores later as a strike force. Enemy spotted at 0800hrs 80 miles from fleet; strike leader orders aircraft to act independently at 0850hrs, and at 0920hrs the command to attack is given. The slow approach of the aircraft allows *Tirpitz* time to manoeuvre and engage; two aircraft are shot down. The attack is not successful but results in the restriction of German capital ships putting to sea if carriers are in the vicinity.

April–July 1942: Convoy duties.

10 August 1942: Passes through Straits of Gibraltar in Operation Pedestal, escorting the convoy to relieve Malta.

12 August 1942: Bomb hits flight deck during heavy air attack, but bounces overboard. Carrier *Eagle* sunk.

15 August 1942: Embarks survivors from *Eagle* at Gibraltar.

16 August 1942: Departs Gibraltar for Rosyth.

21 September 1942: At Scapa Flow for Seafire and Barracuda deck landing trials.

15 October 1942: Sir Winston Churchill and Sir Stafford Cripps (Lord Privy Seal) visit ship.

16 October 1942: Sails for Greenock to embark aircraft.

30 October 1942: Departs Greenock for Operation Torch, as part of Force H, with *Formidable*.

6 November 1942: Enters Mediterranean.

8 November 1942: Aircraft from *Victorious* capture the French military airfield at Blida and attack Algiers and Fort Dupère.

20 December 1942: Sails from Greenock for America.

1–30 January 1943: Refit at Norfolk, Virginia.

3 February 1943: Sails from Norfolk, Virginia, for Panama Canal.

4 March 1943: Arrives at Pearl Harbor, Hawaii.

9 March–8 April 1943: Additional AA armament fitted.

8 May 1943: Sails in company with USS *North Carolina* for exercises with USS *Saratoga*.

9 August 1943: Arrives at Pearl Harbor.

12 August 1943: Departs Pearl Harbor for San Diego.

25 August 1943: Leaves Pacific via Panama Canal.

4 January–3 February 1944: Refit at Liverpool.

17 February–4 March 1944: Refit at Liverpool.

3 April 1944: Operation Tungsten.

5 July 1944: Arrives at Colombo with *Indomitable*.

22 July 1944: Leaves Trincomalee as part of Force 62 for attacks on Lhonga and Kotraja airfields and Sabang Harbour.

25 August 1944: Air attacks on Padang and Emmahaven.

18 September 1944: Attack on Sigli.

17–19 October 1944: Attacks on Nicobar Islands.

25 January 1945: Palembang attack, consisting of 110 aircraft.

29 January 1945: Attacks against Japanese oil refineries at Soengei Gerong.

10 February 1945: Arrives at Sydney, Australia.

28 February 1945: Sails for Manus in Admiralty Islands.

23 March 1945: Assigned to US 5th Fleet.

26 March–2 April 1945: Attacks against Sakishima Gunto airfields.

1 April 1945: First Kamikaze attack on *Victorious*.

12 April 1945: Attacks against airfields in Formosa.

13 April 1945: Attacks against Matsuyama and Shinchiku.

1 May 1945: Attacks against Sakishima Gunto.

9 May 1945: Two Kamikaze hits on *Victorious*; three killed, nineteen wounded, flight deck holed but still operational.

5 June 1945: Arrives Sydney for repairs.

17 July 1945: Minor strikes against airfields at Kyusha.

12 August 1945: Sails for Australia.

25 September 1945: Departs Sydney for Portsmouth with ex-POWs.

27 October 1945: Arrives back at Portsmouth.

31 October 1945: Sails for Plymouth to begin operations as troopship, making three trips to Australia and the Far East during the following 18 months.

14 January 1947: Arrives at Plymouth; became category B reserve two days later.

14 July 1947: Departs Plymouth for Portsmouth and alterations to training ship.

October 1947–March 1950: Part of Portland Training Squadron.

10 October 1950: Taken into Dockyard hands at Portsmouth for modernisation.

14 January 1958: Recommissioned after seven-year refit costing £20,000,000 – the largest operation of its kind undertaken to date.

SUMMARY OF CAREER AFTER MODERNISATION

3 February 1958: Sea trials.

23 June 1958: First deck landing of the Supermarine Scimitar, an aircraft capable of nuclear strike.

28 September 1958: Sails for the Mediterranean.

13 October 1958: Arrives at Malta.

14 January 1959: Returns to Portsmouth.

20 February 1959: Departs on visit to Europe. Takes part in Home Fleet Spring Cruise to the Mediterranean with *Eagle* and *Centaur*.

10 July 1959: Arrives in Norfolk, Virginia, to demonstrate the Type 984 radar and take part in exercise Riptide with US 2nd Fleet.

Late Autumn 1959: Takes part in NATO exercise Blue Frost off Norway. One of her Skyraider aircraft crashes in the sea, but the crew is rescued by a Russian spy trawler covering the exercise.

16 January 1960: Initial deck landing trials of the new Buccaneer aircraft.

26 February–15 August 1960: Refit in D lock at Portsmouth.

14 September 1960: Combined recommissioning and 21st Anniversary of the ship's launching.

18 October 1960: Sails from Portsmouth for Mediterranean.

24–26 October 1960: Alongside at Gibraltar.

4 November 1960: Arrives at Malta.

5 November 1960: Hoists the flag of Rear Admiral R M Smeeton, Flag Officer Aircraft Carriers, who has transferred from *Ark Royal*.

15 November 1960: Sails for second work-up period south of Malta. An AEW Gannet aircraft and crew are lost from 849B Flight.

25 November 1960: Visits Naples.

29 November 1960: Sails for third work-up of three major exercises. The first is *Royal Flush IV*, with *Hermes*, *Ark Royal* and USS *Saratoga*, *Independence* and *Intrepid*.

3 December 1960: *Ark Royal* and *Victorious* take part in exercise Pink Gin III, an Army support exercise off Tobruk.

6 December 1960: The two carriers are joined by *Albion* for exercise Decex, during which a Scimitar ditches after launching from *Victorious*; the pilot is rescued.

10 December 1960: En route for Gibraltar, *Victorious*'s boats and catwalks are damaged by Force Eight gales, and the rudder jammed five degrees to starboard. The ship eventually manages to anchor off Majorca, where divers clear the fouled rudder.

15 December 1960: Arrives off Gibraltar and embarks the First Sea Lord, Admiral Sir Caspar John. Sails for Portsmouth at midnight.

20 January 1961: Departs Portsmouth for Gibraltar.

1 February 1961: Sails from Gibraltar with Flag Officer Aircraft Carriers, with RFA *Tidereach* and HMS *Blackpool*, bound for Cape Town; the three ships became known as 'The Old Vic Touring Company'.

17 February 1961: Enters Cape Town harbour for a ten-day visit and receives an estimated 25,000 visitors.

19 February 1961: The United Kingdom High Commissioner, Sir John Maud, presents a new Queen's Colour to the South American and South Atlantic Station on the flight deck. This is the first time such a ceremony had been performed on a ship; normally this is carried out on sovereign territory.

28 February 1961: Sails from Cape Town.

7 March 1961: Arrives in Aden for a seven-day respite.

14 March 1961: Departs Aden to meet and transfer FOAC to *Hermes*, then proceeds to Singapore.

29 March 1961: Enters Singapore Naval Base.

12 April 1961: Sails to embark squadrons.

19 April 1961: The Flag Officer, 2nd in Command, Rear Admiral Le Fanu, hoists his flag in *Victorious*.

25 April 1961: Joins ships from the US Pacific Fleet to conduct exercises off Borneo. A Scimitar pilot is forced to eject and, although rescued, dies later from his injuries in Changi Hospital.

4 April 1961: Rear Admiral Le Fanu transfers back to *Belfast*.

9 May 1961: Arrives back at Singapore.

16 May 1961: Docks in King George VI dock.

8 June 1961: Ship undocked.

15 June 1961: Sails to embark squadrons and exercise for a week. A Vixen aircraft crashes during night deck landing practice: the crew are lost.

24 June 1961: Returns to Singapore to hoist flag of FO2, Rear Admiral Frewen.

26 June 1961: Sails from Singapore in company with *Tidereach*, *Reliant* and *Resurgent*, the destroyers *Cassandra* and *Carysfort*, and the submarine *Teredo* for exercises en route to Hong Kong.

29 June 1961: Ordered to proceed to Persian Gulf by C-in-C as General Kassem of Iraq threatens to invade Kuwait, newly independent from Britain.

8 July 1961: Arrives in the Gulf of Oman and later in the afternoon enters the Persian Gulf.

9 July 1961: FO2 and his staff transfer to the frigate *Lincoln* to enter Bahrein and confer with the Flag Officer Middle East. Later in the night they return and *Victorious*, *Cassandra* and *Lincoln* head for the Kuwait area. 5000 British troops are ashore, and the naval presence includes *Bulwark* with her Commandos plus three Loch class frigates.

13 July 1961: *Tidereach* and *Reliant* arrive with fuel and stores.

14 July 1961: The ship goes to Action Stations at dawn in anticipation of the Iraqi invasion plans. No invasion takes place, and *Victorious* spends the next two weeks on station.

31 July 1961: *Centaur* arrives to relieve *Victorious*, and FO2 transfers to her. By 1600hrs *Victorious* is heading down the Gulf with *Camperdown* for Mombasa.

21 August 1961: Leaves Mombasa for Aden.

29 August 1961: Arrives off Aden.

2 September 1961: Sails for Singapore with *Reliant*, *Olna* and *Yarmouth*, to be joined by *Blackpool* on the 7th.

15 September 1961: Arrives at Singapore for three weeks maintenance.

5 October 1961: Sails for exercises, leaving the Singapore area on the 13th for Hong Kong.

17 October 1961: Enters Hong Kong harbour at 0930hrs to moor at No 1 buoy, as the ship is too large to go alongside.

25 October 1961: Sails to join USS *Ticonderoga* for exercise Crosstie.

28 October 1961: Berths in Subic Bay.

31 October 1961: Exercises come to a close; one Vixen is lost and another

damaged, but there are no fatalities.

4 September 1961: Back in Singapore.

14 November 1961: Sails for Aden.

16 November 1961: Diverted to Mombasa to render assistance to flood victims.

22 November 1961: Berths alongside at Mombasa. 825 Squadron's helicopter flew up country in the evening to start relief work.

23 November 1961: Sails again for Aden and then Suez.

1 December 1961: Meets *Centaur* in the Gulf of Suez to transfer 824 Squadron and receive FOAC and his staff.

2 December 1961: Enters the Canal at first light with some apprehension as she has not used it before and may be too big. The Canal is successfully negotiated by 1900hrs.

7 December 1961: Bad weather disrupts exercise Royal Flush V with US Sixth Fleet for a day.

18 December 1961: Anchors at Spithead, berthing at South Railway Jetty the following day.

5 February 1962: Sails to embark squadrons the following day.

15–19 February 1962: Visit to Brest.

1–13 March 1962: Self-maintenance period at Gibraltar.

19 March 1962: Start of a four day visit to Vigo, preceded by trials with 1st Destroyer Squadron.

26–29 March 1962: Exercise Dawn Breeze with NATO forces.

2 April 1962: Return to Portsmouth to prepare for extended refit until 12 June 1963. During this refit, two of her after 3in mountings are removed to make way for extra accommodation, and her sextuple Bofors is also landed. The mirror sights are replaced by projector sights and her flyco position is altered; outboard of the island superstructure a mobile equipment and weapons handling platform and servicing position are added.

In 1964 she responded to invasion threats against Malaysia by Indonesia, and visited Australia and Singapore, where a new crew was flown out to the ship. She remained East of Suez until mid-1965, when she returned home for another refit.

7 April 1966: Commissioned at Portsmouth after a £2,500,000 refit.

8 July 1966: Sails from Portsmouth for East of Suez, to relieve the carrier *Eagle*.

28 July 1966: Transits Suez Canal.

23 September 1966: Arrives at Hong Kong.

7 October 1966: Wessex HAS1 helicopter crashes, killing four of the crew.

27 October 1966: Enters Sydney Harbour, Australia, for a twelve-day visit during which a Firefly aircraft is purchased – a survivor of the Korean War – for the Fleet Air Arm Museum at Yeovilton.

21 June 1967: Returns to Portsmouth.

11 November 1967: A fire breaks out in the CPOs' mess No 13 on 2 deck, caused by a faulty hot water urn; one rating is killed. The fire did not cause extensive damage and the ship seems to be recovering well from the incident.

23 November 1967: The Captain is informed the ship will not recommission.

24 November 1967: The recommissioning service is held as a wake for the ship and attended by six former captains.

13 March 1968: *Victorious* finally ends her career, and is sold for scrap in July 1968.

11 July 1969: Departs Portsmouth for the last time and is towed to Scotland Shipbreaking Industries Yard at Faslane to be broken up.

Full speed ahead, *c.* 1963. The flat plate of the UHF/DF aerial on the angled mast and the position formerly occupied by the bridle catcher are clearly visible.
Fleet Photographic Unit

1. *Victorious c.* 1941; the ramps around her catapult on the port side of the flight deck can clearly be seen while steam is also visible emanating from the ejection outlet.
Imperial War Museum

2. *Victorious* leaving Hvalfjord, Iceland, on 4 October 1941, with two Fulmar aircraft on deck. The slope of the island up to A deck is revealed in the dark patch of camouflage below the funnel.
US National Archives

3. *Victorious* at anchor. The Typhoon whistle is visible under the flight deck round down forward, and the noses of two Fulmars and an Albacore can also be seen. Note also the smaller inboard yardarm under the Type 72 DM homing beacon on the foremast.
H W Page

4. *Victorious*, with *Argus* in the background, in the Mediterranean. Just aft of the forward starboard 4.5in guns a Hurricane is parked on an out-rigger.
CMP

5. Looking down the after starboard side of the flight deck, this view shows one of the HADCTs between the two raised W/T transmitting masts. Also visible are fittings for extra arrester wires in the foreground; the original six can be seen aft of these.
H W Page

6. The island superstructure after January 1943: the Type 72 DM homing beacon has been removed from the tripod mast and replaced by the US Navy YE aerial, which can be seen to the left of the mast. In front of the HADCT is the Type 272 radar lantern, and a MF/DF frame has been fitted to the front of the bridge.
H W Page

7. Operating with the US Navy during 1943, *Victorious* shows Wildcats and Avengers parked about the deck, which has been painted with a disruptive pattern to disguise the vulnerable aircraft lifts. *Imperial War Museum*

8. A photograph taken after *Victorious*'s March 1944 refit at Liverpool: the bridge HADCT has been moved down to the former position of the second pom-pom, and a Type 277 radar replaces the Type 272. A new tripod mainmast has been installed to carry Type 293 and a Type 281B radar, and the ship now has a new camouflage scheme. *Imperial War Museum*

9. *Victorious* now wears the colours of the British Pacific Fleet, photographed sometime in 1945, possibly in Australia. The stern gun platform is clearly visible with its twin and single Oerlikons. Corsairs and an Avenger are on deck.
Royal Navy Museum, Portsmouth

10, 11, 12. *Victorious* returning to Portsmouth on 27 October 1945. These pictures show the further additions to the ship's AA armament especially around the island superstructure. She is carrying Seafires and flying a paying-off pendant.
Wright and Logan

13. A Firefly aircraft from the French carrier *Arromanches* causes some distraction as it passes overhead on 8 July 1949. The masts and aerials are much as they were at the end of the war, though the YE homing beacon had been removed from its aerial over the funnel. Two Boffin guns are situated below the bridge.
CMP

14, 15. These two pictures were taken on 2 January 1958, as the ship prepared to commission on the 14th. The stern view reveals the catwalks under the flight deck. In the other the considerable overhang of the angled flight deck can be appreciated, and this view also shows the deck landing mirror sight and platform.
CMP (14) Naval Institute Press (15)

16,17. Two aerial shots of the ship carrying out Gannet AEW3 landing trials during October 1959, when trials for the Sea Vixen Mk 1 took place. Note the triangular deck parking space around the island, made available by the angled flight deck. Two Sea Vixens can be seen at the forward end of the axial deck.
Fleet Air Arm Museum

30

18. *Victorious* entering New York Harbour
in 1959, carrying Scimitars, Sea Venoms
and Skyraiders.
Fleet Photographic Unit

32

19. An impressive view of *Victorious*
turning to starboard, *c*1959.
Fleet Photographic Unit

20. 'Tail-down', a Scimitar is ready for launching. Above the bridge is the massive Type 984 radar with its Mk 10 IFF aerial on top.
FAA Museum

21. *Victorious* entering Grand Harbour, Malta, on 4 November 1960. She has now been fitted with a bridle catcher for the port catapult; this was fitted only until the end of 1961.
John G Callis

22. *Victorious* in July 1963, with a mobile equipment and weapons platform added outboard of the island and one of her after 3in mounts replaced by extra accommodation and 250 gallon LOX tanks for the Buccaneers she would now be operating.
Wright and Logan

23. A stern view of *Victorious* at Portsmouth on 25 August 1965, prior to going into dry dock for a refit.
John G Callis

24. *Victorious* arriving at Valetta, Malta, on 20 July 1966, showing the Buccaneer drop tank stowage, extra accommodation where the 3in mount used to be, and the deck landing projector sight.
CMP

25. *Victorious* laid up in Fareham Lake, Portsmouth, in June 1969. She has been stripped of her fittings and is awaiting scrap.
Mike Lennon

26. *Victorious* under tow to the breakers on 15 July 1969.
Maritime Photo Library

THE DRAWINGS

A General arrangement

A1 **EXTERNAL APPEARANCE AS COMPLETED, APRIL 1941**

(All drawings in section A are to 1/550 scale)

A1/1 Starboard profile

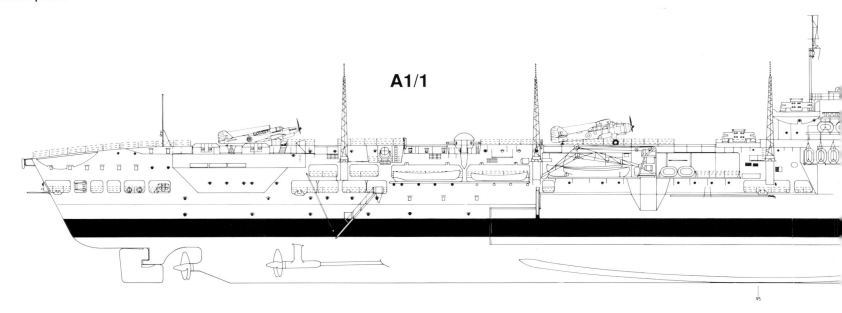

A1/1

A1/2 Port profile

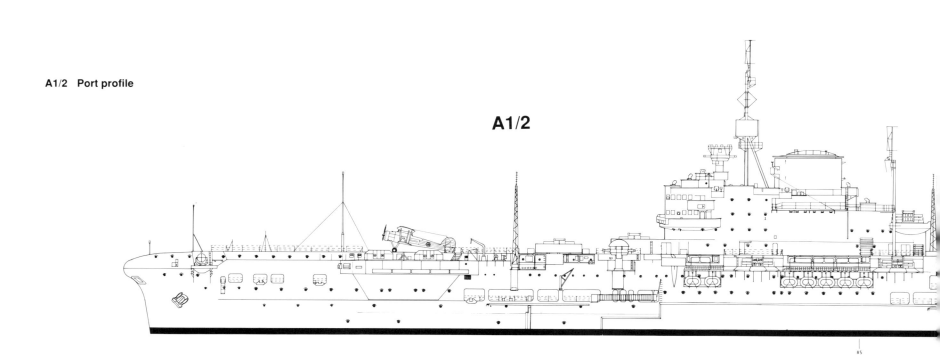

A1/2

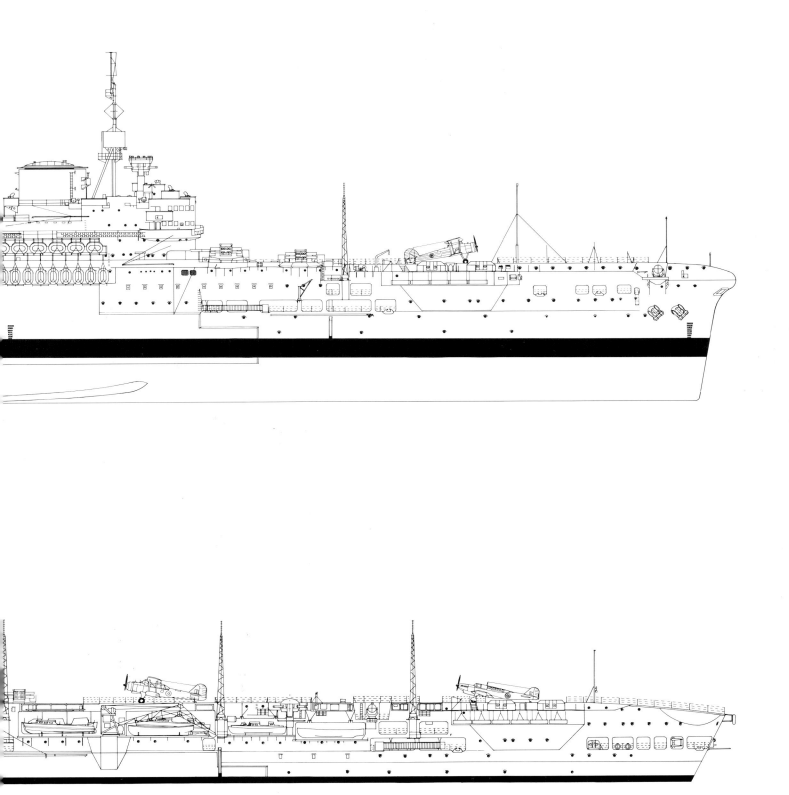

A General arrangement

A2 INTERNAL ARRANGEMENTS 1941

A2/1 Internal profile

1. FAA maintenance store
2. Lt Cdr (F)'s office
3. Lobby
4. Aircraft lift
5. Hangar armoured sliding door
6. Hangar
7. After control platform
8. No 2 squadron lay apart store
9. No 2 squadron armament ready-use store
10. No 5 flight store
11. Spare store room
12. Parachute packing room
13. No 2 W/T ready-use store
14. Torpedo lift cover machinery
15. Admiral's sleeping cabin
16. Admiral's flat
17. Cinema projection room
18. Balance weight trunk
19. Quarterdeck
20. Officers' baggage room
21. Wardroom officers' WCs
22. Wardroom officers' urinals
23. Capstan machinery room
24. Officers' sleeping berths
25. Portable bilge pump flat
26. Ammunition hand winding gear regulator flat
27. Ammunition hoist flat
28. Ammunition Conveyor flat
29. Dental surgery
30. Laundry
31. Torpedo trolley flat
32. Torpedo parting room
33. Boiler uptakes
34. Cabin flat
35. Officer's cabin
36. Link trainer compartment
37. Main naval store
38. Fire control workshop
39. Gyro compass
40. Engineers' lub oil tank
41. Centre machine shop
42. Fan space
43. Bomb lift machinery
44. No 3 petrol control room
45. Airspace

46. Tiller flat
47. Steering gear store
48. Admiral's store
49. No 4 provision room
50. Fresh water tank
51. Officers' bedding store
52. Marines' store
53. No 1 naval store
54. 4.5in magazine
55. Watertight trunk
56. Centre engine room
57. Main feed tank
58. Machinery control room
59. Bomb lift
60. Bomb room
61. Centre boiler room
62. Engineers' spare gear store
63. Wardroom wine store
64. Wardroom store
65. 75-ton fire and ballast pump room
66. After LP compressor room
67. Centre gland space
68. Plummer block compartment
69. Fireworks magazine
70. No 1 warhead room
71. 150-ton pump room
72. Boiler room vent
73. Passage
74. Airlock
75. Servery

76. RDF power room
77. No 2 Flight store
78. No 5 naval store
79. Spare engine store
80. Forward control platform
81. Assisted take-off gear platform
82. FAA mess
83. Seamens' mess
84. Stokers' mess
85. Ship's company urinals
86. Decontamination store
87. Crew's recreation space
88. Lecture room school and library
89. Gymnastic gear store
90. Cable gear store
91. Aircraft repair shop
92. CPOs' and POs' WCs and urinals
93. Ship's company WCs and urinals
94. Lamp room
95. Electric lead passage
96. No 1 W/T power supply room
97. POs' washplace
98. Cable locker flat
99. Paint room
100. Spare anchor gear store
101. Reserve feed tank
102. No 2 petrol control compartment
103. Medical distribution station
104. FAA cloakroom
105. Oilskin and seaboot store

106. Crew's cloakroom
107. No 2 naval store
108. No 2 flour store
109. Soap clothing and tobacco store
110. Clothing issue room
111. Canvas and awning store
112. Cable locker
113. Paint store
114. Petrol tank compartment
115. Empty practice bomb room
116. Detonator compartment
117. Spirit room
118. CO_2 machinery compartment
119. Cold room
120. Inflammables store
121. Pom-pom magazine
122. Pitometer log compartment
123. Turbo hydraulic pump room for assisted take-off gear
124. Forward spare armature store

a. Flight deck
b. Upper gallery deck
c. Lower gallery deck
d. Hangar deck
e. Upper deck
f. Main deck
g. Lower deck
h. Platform deck
i. Hold

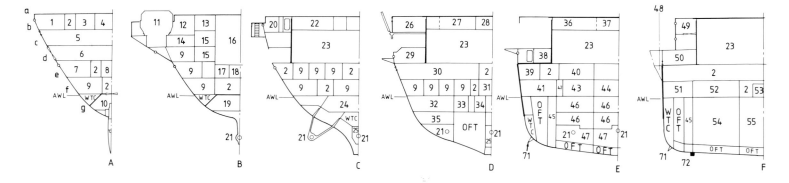

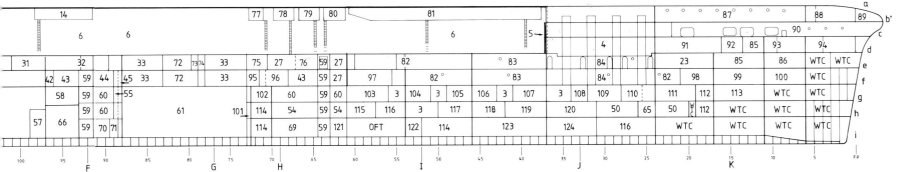

A2/2 Transverse sections

1	Admiral's galley
2	Lobby
3	No 1 squadron office
4	No 2 squadron office
5	Admiral's dining cabin
6	Quarterdeck
7	Band instrument room
8	Capstan machinery compartment
9	Cabin
10	Tiller flat
11	4.5in HA/LA twin mounting
12	Gunbay
13	Lift motor room
14	Gunners' ready-use store
15	Passage
16	Aircraft lift
17	Quarterdeck locker
18	Officers' baggage room
19	Steering gear compartment store
20	Aircraft armament workshop and store
21	Propeller shaft
22	Deep beam at hangar door
23	Hangar
24	Provision room
25	Plummer block compartment
26	Wardroom galley
27	No 3 squadron lay apart store
28	No 2 squadron lay apart store
29	Marines' mess
30	Wardroom
31	Link trainer compartment
32	Implement store
33	Breaker room
34	Warrant officers' store
35	Spare armature store
36	No 4 flight store
37	No 5 flight store
38	Stoker POs' pantry
39	Transmitter room
40	Shipwright's workshop
41	Oil-fuel working space
42	Electric lead passage
43	Transmitter station
44	Fire control workshop
45	Air space
46	4.5in magazine
47	Small arms magazine
48	Crane post centreline
49	Motor boat engine store
50	Stoker POs' mess
51	Marines' washplace
52	Engineers' test room
53	Engineers' lub-oil tank
54	Starboard engine room
55	Centre engine room
56	2pdr pom-pom platform
57	Air gunners' kit store
58	Balloon filling station
59	RDF office
60	W/T mast pump room
61	Torpedo body parting space
62	Aircraft lub-oil store
63	Turbo-generator room
64	Bomb lift machinery
65	Pom-pom magazine
66	Steam pipe passage
67	Bomb room
68	Petrol tank compartment
69	Warhead and bomb room
70	Warhead room
71	Bilge keel
72	Docking keel
73	Charthouse
74	Meteorological office
75	Flying control room
76	Admiral's bathroom
77	Naval store
78	FAA ready-use small arms magazine
79	Officers' urinals and WCs
80	Ship's galley
81	Mechanicians' and chief stokers' mess
82	W/T power supply
83	Switchboard room
84	Fireworks magazine
85	Deep beam
86	Vegetable store
87	Ship's kitchen
88	FAA mess
89	FAA cloakroom
90	Loan bedding store
91	General mess store
92	Balance weight trunk
93	FAA acid and battery store
94	Ordnance spares
95	Issue room
96	Stokers' mess
97	Flour store
98	Dope and acetone room
99	Crew's recreation space
100	Ice cream and soda fountain
101	CPOs' recreation space
102	CPOs' and POs' WCs
103	Aero engine stripping shop
104	Crew's urinals and WCs
105	Paint room
106	Paint store

a	Flight deck
b	Upper gallery
c	Lower gallery
d	Hangar deck
e	Upper deck
f	Main deck
g	Lower deck
h	Platform deck
i	Hold
A	A deck
B	B deck
C	C deck
D	D deck

A2/2

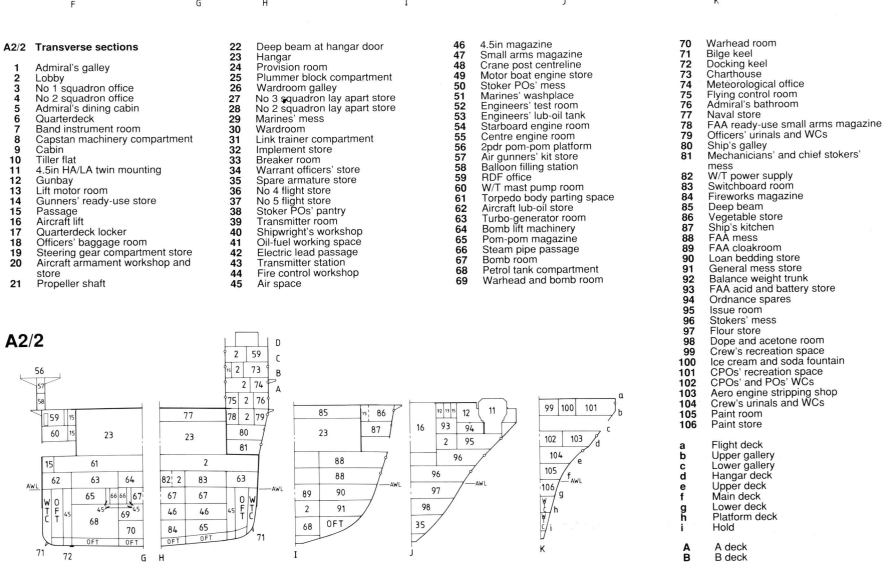

A General arrangement

A3 DECKS

A3/1 Tank top

1 Plummer block compartment
2 Overflow feed tank

OFT Oil fuel tank
WTC Water-tight compartment

A3/1

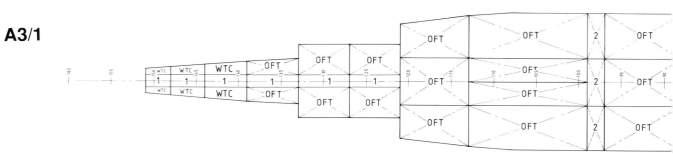

A3/2 Hold

1 Centre gland space
2 Plummer block compartment
3 Port gland and plummer block compartment
4 Starboard gland and plummer block compartment
5 Fireworks magazine
6 Airspace
7 Small arms magazine
8 Port engine room
9 Centre engine room
10 Starboard engine room
11 Evaporating machinery compartment
12 After LP compressor room
13 Petrol tank compartment
14 Bomb lift
15 Warhead room

16 150-ton pump room
17 Port boiler room
18 Centre boiler room
19 Starboard boiler room
20 Pom-pom magazine
21 Sullage tank
22 Sullage pump room flat (over)
23 Oil fuel settling tank
24 Recovery tanks
25 75-ton pump room
26 Pitometer log compartment
27 Assisted take-off gear turbo-hydraulic pump room
28 Forward spare armature store
29 Detonator compartment

WTC Water-tight compartment
OFT Oil fuel tank
RFT Reserve feed tank

A3/2

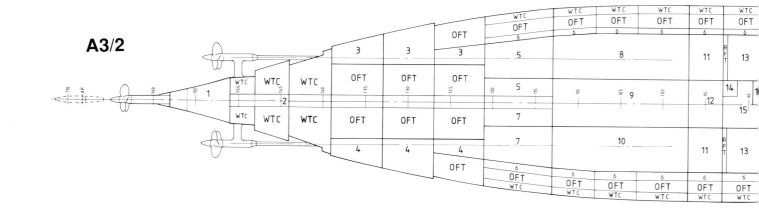

OFT OFT OFT OFT OFT OFT OFT

OFT OFT OFT OFT OFT WTC WTC WTC WTC WTC WTC WTC F.P.

OFT OFT OFT OFT OFT

WTC WTC WTC
OFT OFT OFT WTC WTC
OFT OFT
22 23 24
17 13 5 20 16 OFT
RFT OFT
5 20 OFT 25 13
13 14 27 28 29 WTC WTC WTC F.P.
18 RFT 5 OFT 26 13
13 20 20 16 OFT OFT
19 21
OFT OFT OFT OFT OFT
OFT OFT OFT WTC
WTC WTC WTC

43

A General arrangement

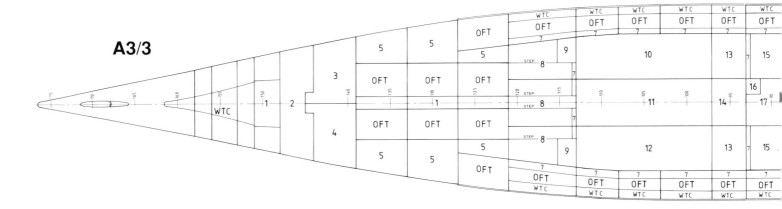

A3/3

A3/3 Platform deck

1   Engineers' spare gear store
2   Wardroom wine store
3   Wardroom store
4   Provision room
5   Naval store
6   After spare armature store
7   Air space
8   4.5in magazine
9   150-ton pump and plummer block
    compartment

10 Port engine room
11 Centre engine room
12 Starboard engine room
13 Evaporating machinery compartment
14 After LP compressor room
15 Petrol tank compartment
16 Bomb lift
17 Warhead boiler room
18 Port boiler room
19 Centre boiler room
20 Starboard boiler room
21 Watertight trunk

22 Crown of 150-ton pump room
23 Sullage tank pump room
24 Oil fuel recovery and settling tank
    room
25 Oil-tight trunk
26 Empty practice bomb room
27 No 2 detonator compartment
28 Sullage tank
29 Canteen store
30 Lobby
31 Spirit room
32 Petrol control compartment

33 General mess store
34 CO$_2$ machinery compartment
35 Cold room
36 Airlock
37 Officers' cold room
38 Imflammables room
39 Dope and acetone room
40 Fresh water tank
41 75-ton pump room
42 Cable locker

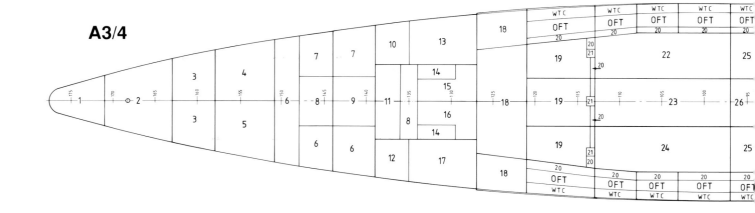

A3/4

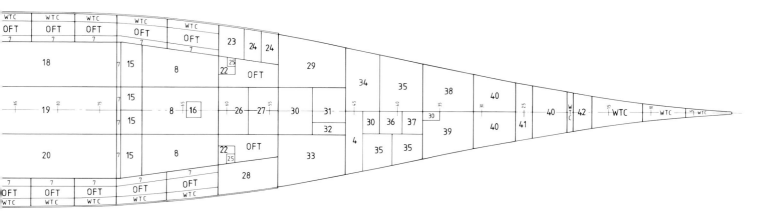

A3/4 Lower deck

1	Officers' baggage room	13	Ship's armament store	27	Pom-pom magazine	41	POs' cloakroom

1   Officers' baggage room
2   Tiller flat
3   Steering gear store
4   Admiral's store
5   Captain's store
6   Provision room
7   Flour store
8   Lobby
9   Fresh water tank
10 Marines' great coat store
11 Officers' bedding store
12 Chart and chronometer room

13 Ship's armament store
14 Breaker room
15 Marines' store
16 Warrant officers' store
17 Paymaster's store
18 Naval store
19 4.5in magazine
20 Airspace
21 Watertight trunk
22 Port engine room
23 Centre engine room
24 Starboard engine room
25 Evaporating machinery room
26 Machinery control room

27 Pom-pom magazine
28 Bomb lift
29 Bomb room
30 Port boiler room
31 Centre boiler room
32 Starboard boiler room
33 Passage
34 EL store and working space
35 EL cloakroom
36 POs' baggage room
37 Medical distributing station
38 Medical store
39 Ship's armament store
40 Crew's cloakroom

41 POs' cloakroom
42 Photographic room
43 Developing room
44 Light trap
45 Photographic office
46 FAA cloakroom
47 Oilskin and seaboot store
48 Loan bedding store
49 Soap clothing and tobacco store
50 Canvas and awning store
51 Cable locker
52 Paint store

A General arrangement

A3/5

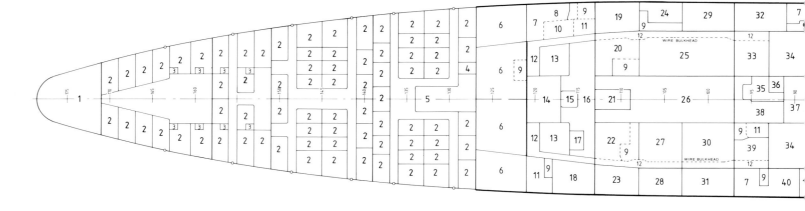

A3/5 Main deck

1	Officers' baggage room
2	Officer's cabin
3	Balance weight trunk
4	Confidential book cupboard
5	Link trainer compartment
6	Main naval store
7	Oil fuel working space
8	Oxygen store
9	Lobby
10	Type 282 and 285 power supply
11	W/T power supply
12	Electric lead passage
13	HA/LA calculating position
14	Fire control workshop
15	Gyro compass
16	4.5in ammunition lobby
17	DB store
18	Low pressure supply room
19	High pressure supply room
20	Engineers' ready-use store
21	Engineers' lub-oil tank
22	Engineers' test room
23	Marines' washplace
24	Torpedo electricians' store
25	Port machine shop
26	Centre machine shop
27	Engineers' fitting shop
28	ERAs' dressing room
29	Fireworks magazine
30	Starboard machine shop
31	ERAs' washplace
32	Torpedo lifting compartment
33	EAs' fitting shop
34	Turbo-generator room
35	Bomb lift machinery
36	Bomb lift
37	Petrol control compartment
38	Fan compartment
39	OAs' fitting shop
40	Aircraft lub-oil store
41	Boiler uptake
42	Dwarf bulkhead
43	Boiler room fan space
44	Drying room
45	Watertight trunk
46	Airspace
47	LP air compressor room
48	Soot plant
49	Firebrick store
50	Stokers' dressing room
51	Stokers' washplace
52	HA calculating position
53	Switchboard room
54	HA/LA calculating room
55	Lower steering position
56	Telephone exchange
57	LP supply and gyro compass room
58	Seamen's and FAA washplace
59	CPOs' washplace
60	POs' washplace
61	FAA mess
62	Seamen's mess
63	Stokers' mess
64	Cable locker
65	Paint room
66	Spare anchor gear store

A3/6

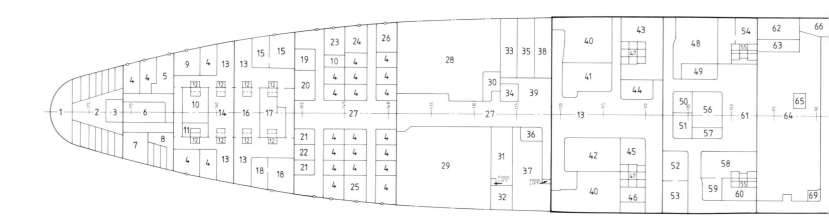

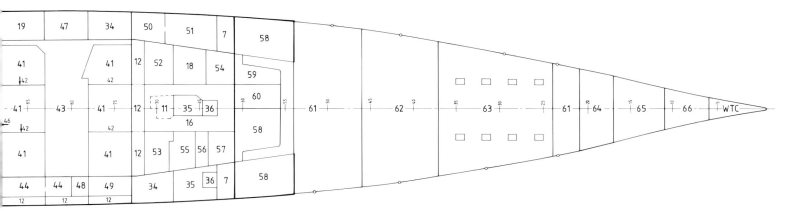

A3/6 Upper deck

1 Baggage room
2 Wardroom officers' WCs
3 Wardroom officers' urinals
4 Officer's cabin
5 Royal marine officer's cabin
6 Capstan machinery room
7 Band instrument room
8 Wardroom officers' WCs and urinals
9 Lieutenant commander flying officer's cabin
10 Sleeping berths for officers
11 DG store
12 Balance weight trunk
13 Ammunition hoist trunk
14 Portable bilge pump flat
15 Commander engineer's cabin
16 Ammunition hand winding gear feed regulator flat
17 Officers' baggage room
18 Pay office
19 Gunnery office
20 Torpedo office
21 Commander gunner's cabin
22 Commander supply officer's cabin
23 Senior engineer officer's cabin
24 Chaplain's cabin
25 Squadron leader's cabin

26 Navigating officer's cabin
27 Ammunition conveyor flat
28 Wardroom ante-room
29 Wardroom
30 Wardroom wine pantry
31 Wardroom pantry
32 Scullery
33 FAA office
34 Commander's office
35 Captain's office
36 Warrant officers' pantry
37 Warrant officers' mess and restroom
38 Engineer's office
39 Motor dynamo flat
40 Transmitting room
41 Naval store office
42 Shipwrights' workshop
43 Wardroom officers' bathroom
44 Warrant officers' bathroom
45 Shipwrights' ready-use store
46 Ship's company's WCs and urinals
47 Engine room exhaust vent
48 Chapel
49 Damage control headquarters
50 Master at arms' office
51 Dental surgery
52 Stoker POs' dressing room
53 Stoker POs' washplace
54 Writers' supply and sick berth

assistants' washplace
55 Engine room supply vent
56 Laundry
57 Iron room
58 Stokers' washplace
59 Stokers' dressing room
60 Officers' stewards' and cooks' washplace
61 Torpedo trolley flat
62 Blowing head compartment
63 Torpedo and bomb lift
64 Torpedo parting room
65 Bomb lift
66 Gunners' ready-use torpedo store
67 Rating pilots' and observers' washplace
68 Boiler uptakes
69 Mess cleaning gear store
70 Washplace
71 Mechanicians' and chief stokers' washplace
72 Mechanicians' and chief stokers' dressing room
73 Boiler room vent
74 Drying room
75 Bakery
76 Bread cooling room
77 Ready-use flour store
78 Servery

79 Passenger lift machinery
80 Central communications office
81 Annexe
82 Canteen
83 Cypher office
84 RDF power room
85 CPOs' naval mess
86 CPOs' pantry
87 DG motor room
88 Bookstall
89 FAAs' mess
90 POs' naval and FAAs' mess
91 POs' pantry
92 Writers' supply and sick berth assistants' mess
93 Seamen's mess
94 Stokers' mess
95 Prison
96 Capstan machinery flat
97 Ship's company's WCs
98 Ship's company's urinals
99 Decontamination store

WTC Watertight compartment

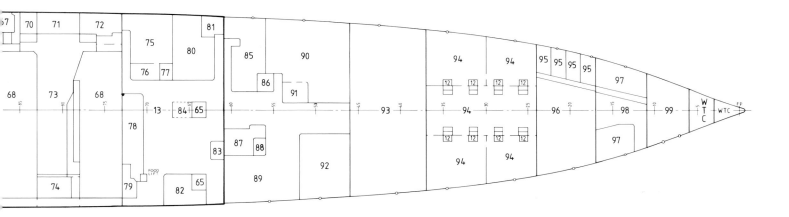

A General arrangement

A3/7

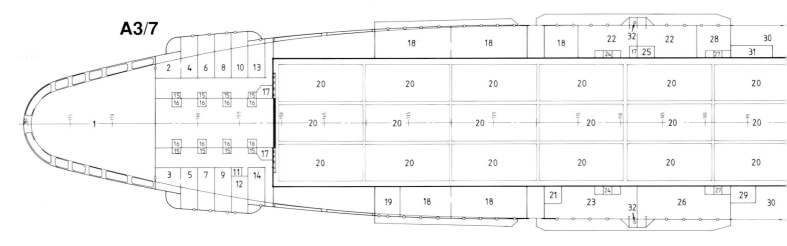

A3/7	Hangar deck	22	Officers' stewards' and cooks' mess	45	Regulating POs' mess
1	Quarterdeck	23	Stoker POs' mess	46	Victualling office
2	Flying commander's office	24	Engine room exhaust vent	47	Boys' instructors' mess
3	Paymaster commander's office	25	Airlock	48	Boys' washplace
4	Flying commander's cabin	26	ERAs' mess	49	Canteen staff mess
5	Paymaster commander's cabin	27	Engine room supply vent	50	Boys' mess
6	Flying lieutenant commander's cabin	28	Rating pilots' and observers' mess	51	Aircraft repair shop
7	Flag lieutenant's cabin	29	ERAs' pantry	52	Aero engine stripping room
8	Lieutenant commander's cabin	30	Hot weather billets	53	CPOs' and POs' WCs and urinals
9	Admiral's secretary's cabin	31	Torpedo lifts	54	Ship's company's urinals
10	Staff office	32	Foot of seaplane crane	55	Office and store
11	Officers' WC	33	Boiler room vent	56	Ablution cabinet
12	Officers' bathroom	34	Funnel uptake	57	Boys' WCs and urinals
13	Air service commander's cabin	35	Incinerator room	58	Ship's company's WCs and urinals
14	Surgeon commander's cabin	36	FAA CPOs' pantry	59	Ship's company's WCs
15	Balance weight trunk	37	Passenger lift	60	Lamp room
16	Buffer recess	38	FAA CPOs' mess	61	Hawse pipe
17	Access lobby	39	Mechanicians' and chief stoker's mess		
18	Marines' mess	40	RDF office		
19	Sergeants', colour sergeants' and buglers' mess	41	Bomb lift		
20	Aircraft stowed position	42	Paravane stowage		
21	Stoker POs' pantry	43	MAA's and mail office		
		44	Issue room		

A3/8

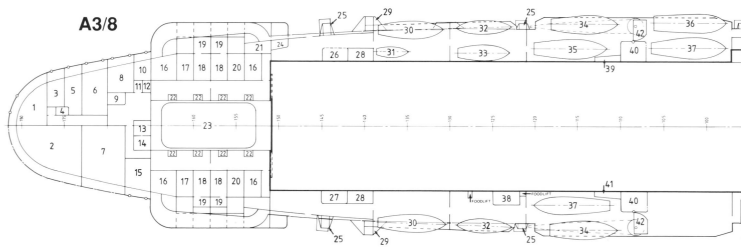

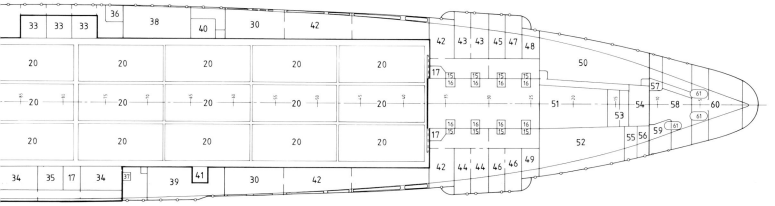

A3/8   Lower gallery deck

1	Admiral's sleeping cabin	22	Balance weight trunk
2	Admiral's day cabin	23	Aircraft lift
3	Admiral's bathroom	24	Coal bunker
4	Admiral's WC	25	Transmitting mast
5	Admiral's spare cabin	26	Shipwrights' ready-use boat store
6	Captain's day cabin	27	Boat gear store
7	Admiral's dining cabin or officers'	28	RDF office
	sleeping quarters	29	Searchlight platform
8	Captain's sleeping cabin	30	32ft life cutter
9	Confidential book office	31	16ft motor dinghy
10	Captain's bathroom	32	27ft whaler
11	Lobby	33	25ft fast motor boat
12	Captain's WC	34	32ft motor cutter
13	Cinema projection room	35	35ft fast motor boat
14	Rewind room	36	35ft fast seaplane tender
15	Admiral's pantry	37	36ft motor pinnace
16	Pump space	38	Diving gear store
17	Gunners' ready-use store	39	Engine room exhaust vent
18	Hoist space	40	Motorboat engine work space
19	Empty cartridge cases	41	Engine room supply vent
20	Seamarker store	42	Electric crane
21	Coke bunker	43	Torpedo lift
		44	Ship's company WCs and urinals
		45	Gyro adjusting room

46	Acid battery store	70	Beef screen
47	Parachute drying room	71	Ordnance spares
48	W/T mast pump room	72	EAs' and OAs' washplace
49	Funnel uptake	73	FAA acid and battery store
50	Boiler room vents	74	Electrical ready-use and paravanes
51	Carley float platform		gear store
52	Consulting room	75	Boswain's ready-use store
53	Operating room	76	Cable deck
54	Surgical dressing room		
55	Passenger lift		
56	Ship's galley		
57	Bomb lift		
58	Surgeon's consulting room		
59	Sick bay		
60	Kitchen		
61	Bathroom		
62	Medical store		
63	Dispensary		
64	WC		
65	Ablution annexe		
66	Isolation ward		
67	Vegetable preparing room		
68	Receiving mast		
69	CPOs' and POs' WCs and urinals		

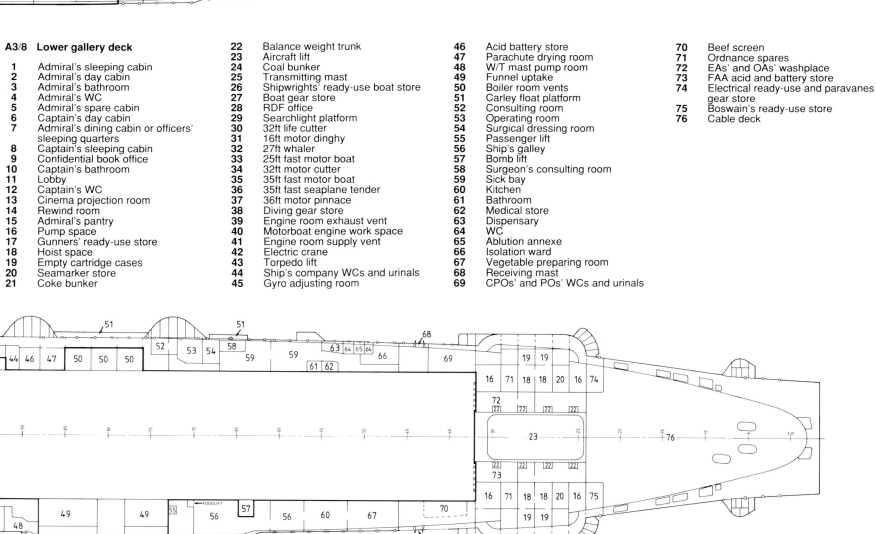

A General arrangement

A3/9

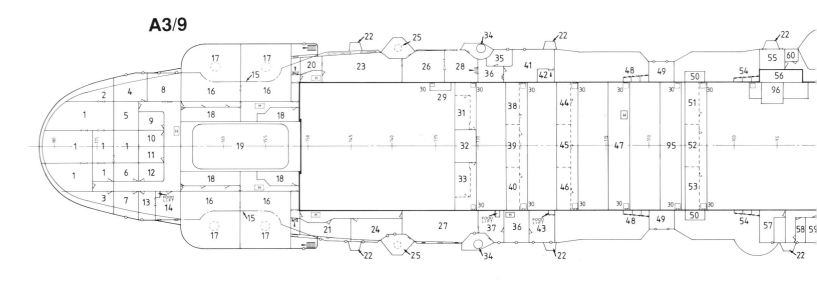

3/9	**Upper gallery deck**	**33**	No 3 squadron lay apart store	**66**	No 3 flight store

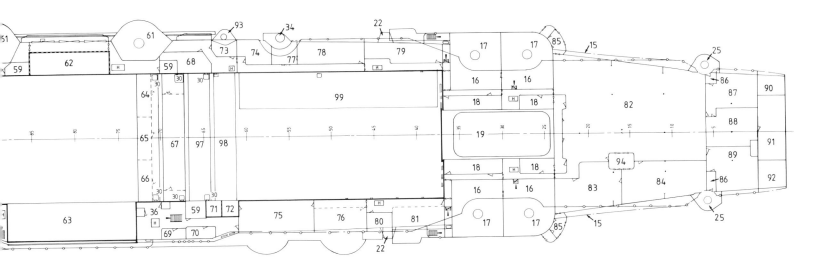

A General arrangement

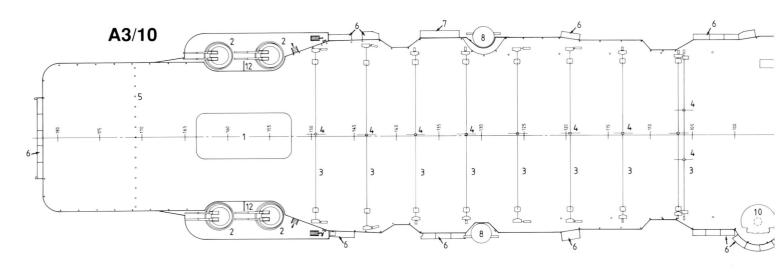

A3/10

A3/10 Flight deck

1	Aircraft lift
2	4.5in HA/LA twin mounting
3	Arresting wire
4	Rope support
5	Round-down lights
6	Safety net
7	Arresting gear control platform
8	HA director tower
9	Torpedo lift cover
10	2pdr multiple pom-pom
11	Wireless lead in for RDF mast
12	Ramp
13	Crash barrier
14	RDF aerial mast
15	Balloon filling station
16	Pilot and observers' waiting room
17	Funnel uptakes
18	Lobby
19	RDF office
20	Admiral's sea cabin
21	Lift
22	WC
23	Bathroom
24	Flying control room
25	Navigating officer's cabin
26	Bomb lift cage
27	Pom-pom director
28	Control gear
29	Assisted take-off gear control panel
30	Direction light
31	1½-ton winch
32	Windscreen

A4   ISLAND SUPERSTRUCTURE

A4/1   Internal profile

A4/2   A deck

A4/3   B deck

A4/4   C deck

A4/5   D deck

A4/6   Signal house top

A4/1

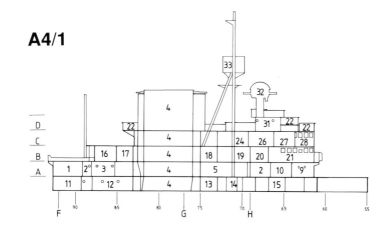

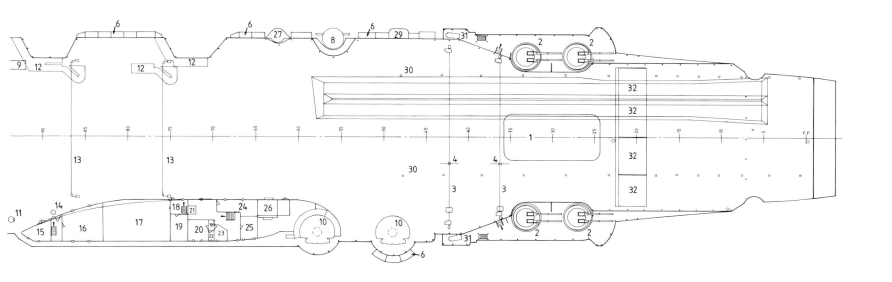

A4/5

A4/6

A4/4

A4/3

A4/2

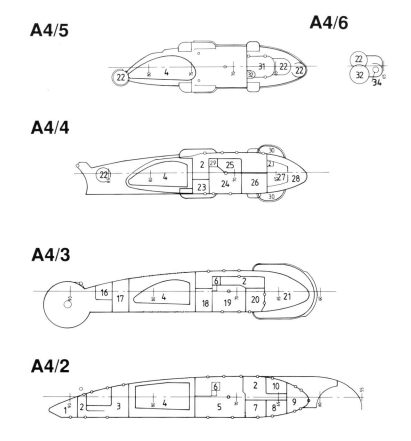

1	Air gunners' kit store
2	Lobby
3	Pilot and observers' kit store and waiting room
4	Funnel uptakes
5	Air operations room
6	Lift
7	Meteorological office
8	Captain's sea cabin
9	Wheelhouse
10	Flying commander's sea cabin
11	Balloon filling station
12	Pilot's and observers' waiting room
13	No 6 RDF office
14	Admiral's sea cabin
15	Navigating officer's cabin
16	Ready-use pom-pom magazine
17	No 7 RDF office
18	No 5 RDF office
19	Plotting office
20	Charthouse
21	Compass platform
22	Pom-pom director
23	Type 72 DM office
24	Remote control office
25	Direction finding office
26	No 1 RDF office
27	Captain's sea cabin
28	Admiral's bridge
29	Ready-use signal store
30	Admiral's viewing platform
31	Signal house
32	HA director tower
33	Type 72 DM apparatus screen
34	Tactical and navigational rangefinder

A General arrangement

A5/1

Light grey

Dark grey

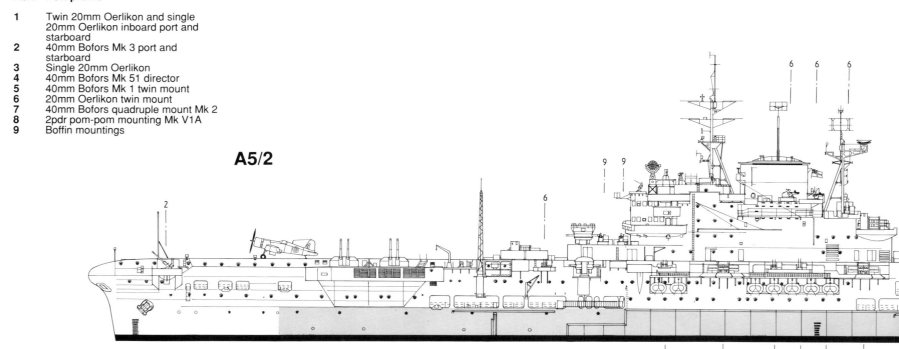

A5/1 Starboard profile

A5/2 Port profile

1   Twin 20mm Oerlikon and single
    20mm Oerlikon inboard port and
    starboard
2   40mm Bofors Mk 3 port and
    starboard
3   Single 20mm Oerlikon
4   40mm Bofors Mk 51 director
5   40mm Bofors Mk 1 twin mount
6   20mm Oerlikon twin mount
7   40mm Bofors quadruple mount Mk 2
8   2pdr pom-pom mounting Mk V1A
9   Boffin mountings

A5/2

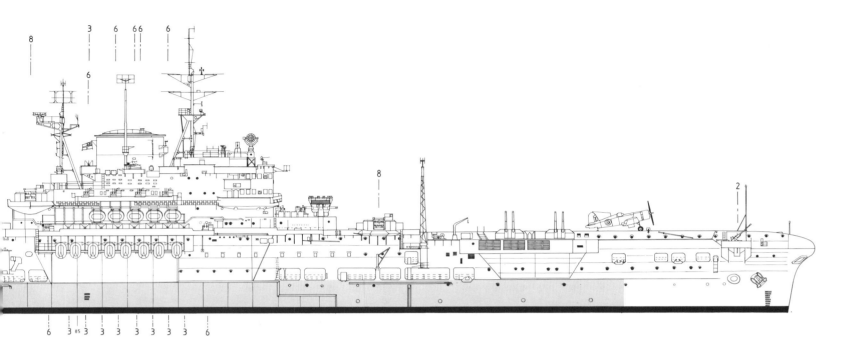

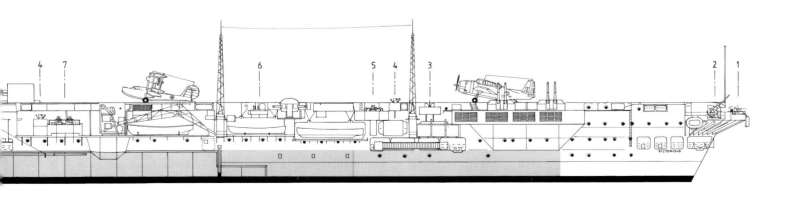

A General arrangement

A6/1

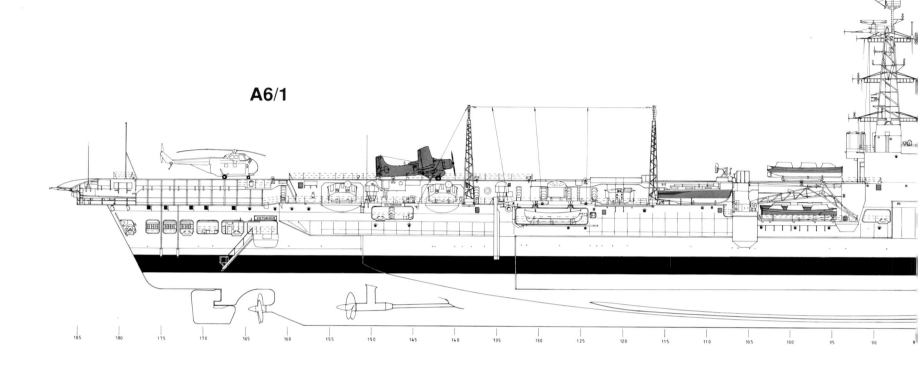

A6/1   Starboard profile

A6/2   Port profile

A6/2

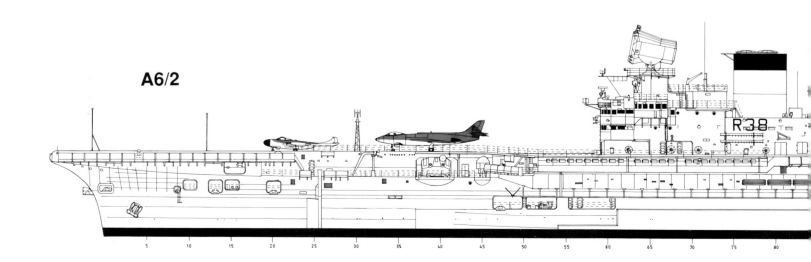

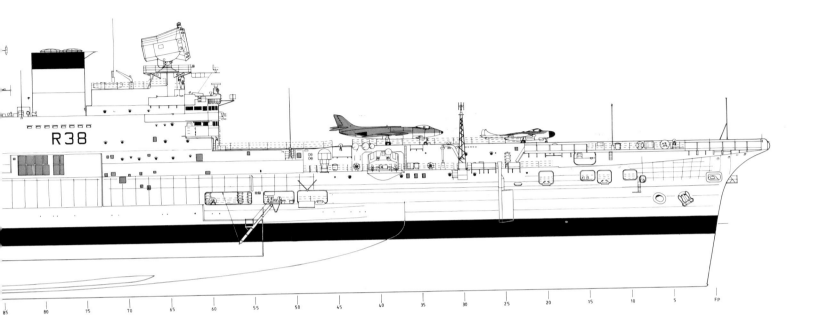

R38

85 80 75 70 65 60 55 50 45 40 35 30 25 20 15 10 5 FP

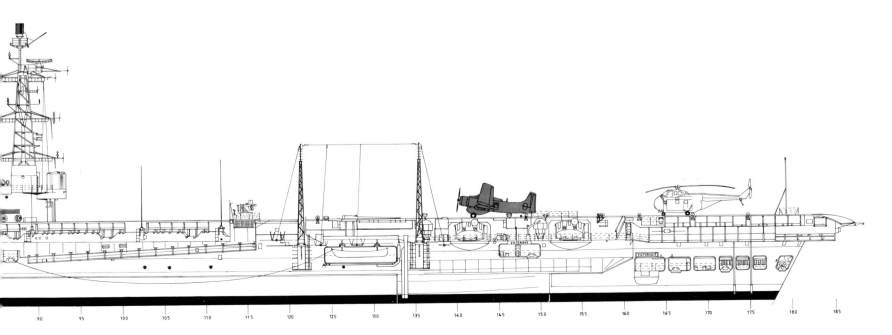

90 95 100 105 110 115 120 125 130 135 140 145 150 155 160 165 170 175 180 185

A General arrangement

A7

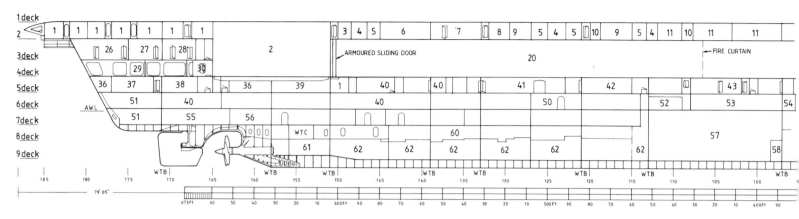

A8/1

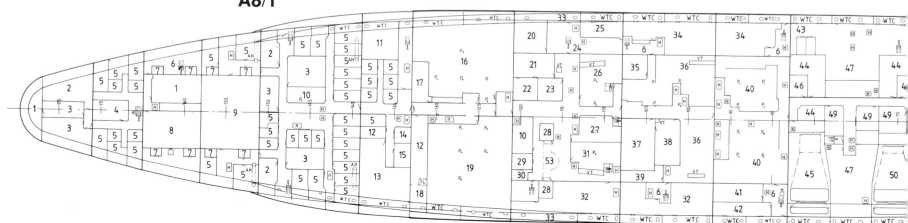

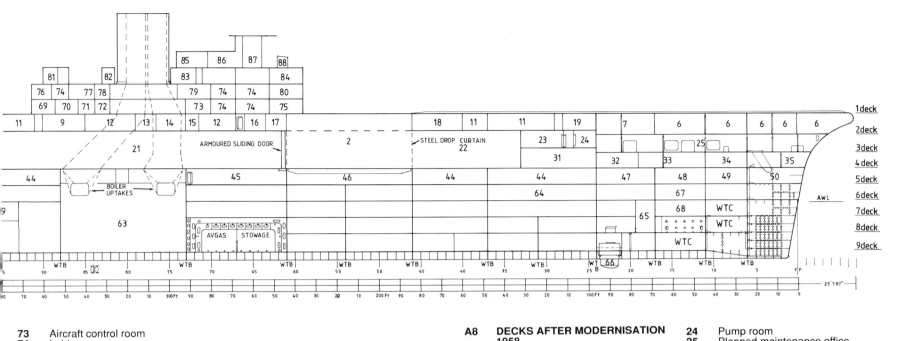

73 Aircraft control room
74 Lobby
75 Flight deck equipment store
76 QPT room
77 293Q radar office
78 Electronic warfare office
79 V-UHF transmitter room
80 Admiral's bridge
81 AEW office (airborne early warning)
82 Visual signalling ready-use store
83 Main signal transmitting room
84 Compass platform
85 Turbo blower and fan compartment
86 Type 984 mounting machine room
87 Type 984 modulator well
88 Air plot shelter

**A8   DECKS AFTER MODERNISATION
1958**

A8/1   Upper deck No 5

1 Officers' baggage store
2 Officers' heads
3 Officers' bathroom
4 Capstan machinery room
5 Officers' cabin
6 Lobby
7 Jigger trunk
8 Air store
9 Lift machinery room
10 USB and damage control base
11 Naval store office
12 Pantry
13 Wardrom annexe
14 Confidential book store
15 Ship's keyboard
16 Wardroom ante-room
17 Wine pantry
18 Scullery
19 Wardroom
20 Lower transmitter room

21 Lower receiver room
22 Cryptographic office
23 Secret cryptographic office

24 Pump room
25 Planned maintenance office
26 Canteen staff's mess
27 Engineers' office
28 Bomb lift
29 Ship's recording equipment room
30 Ship's recording equipment studio
31 Pay office
32 Officers' stewards' and cooks' mess
33 FFO working space
34 Junior rating' mess
35 Emergency operating station
36 Marines' mess
37 Main switchboard
38 HQ1
39 Broadcast compartment
40 Seamen's mess
41 CPOs' and POs' heads
42 Junior ratings' heads
43 Naval store
44 Drying room
45 After boiler uptake
46 Soot removal plant
47 Blower flat
48 Engineer's boiler uptake
49 Engineers' spare gear store
50 Forward boiler uptake
51 Air ratings' mess
52 Ammunition lift
53 Bomb lift platform
54 HQ2
55 Bookstall
56 Canteen
57 Soda fountain bar
58 Catapult jigger trunk
59 Auxiliary rise and fall platform
60 Alkaline battery charging room
61 ABCD workshop
62 Engineering mechanics' mess
63 Cell
64 Forward capstan machinery flat
65 ABCD gear store

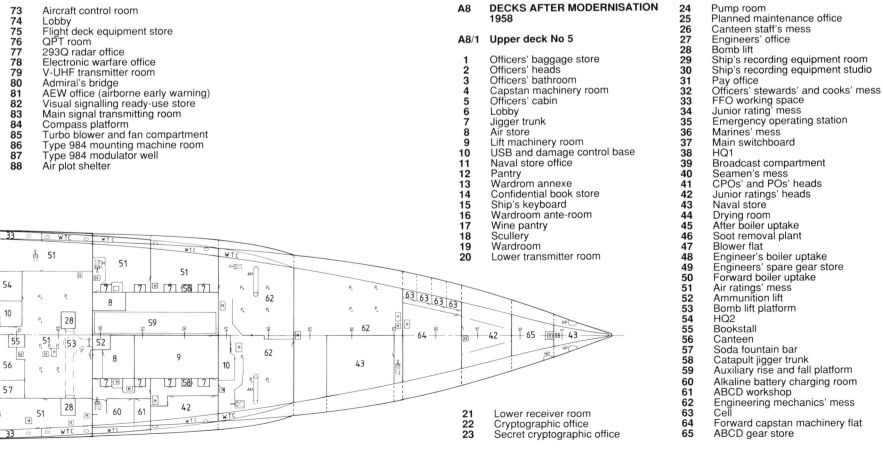

A General arrangement

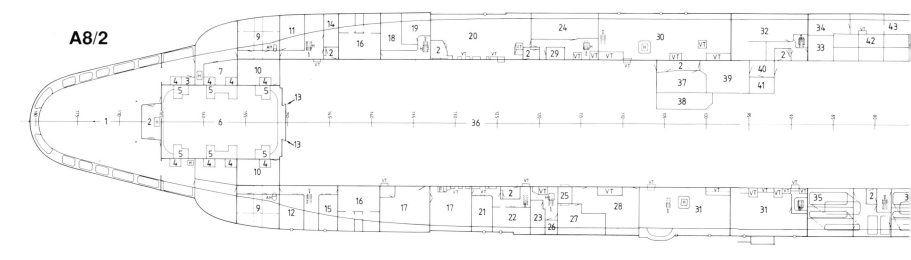

A8/2

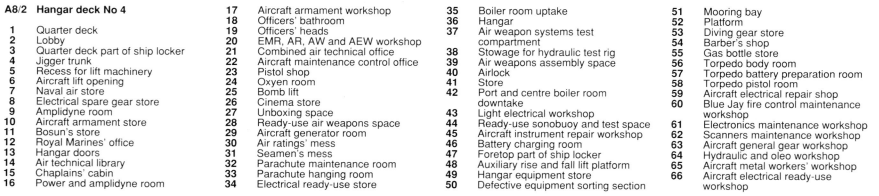

A8/2 Hangar deck No 4

1 Quarter deck
2 Lobby
3 Quarter deck part of ship locker
4 Jigger trunk
5 Recess for lift machinery
6 Aircraft lift opening
7 Naval air store
8 Electrical spare gear store
9 Amplidyne room
10 Aircraft armament store
11 Bosun's store
12 Royal Marines' office
13 Hangar doors
14 Air technical library
15 Chaplains' cabin
16 Power and amplidyne room

17 Aircraft armament workshop
18 Officers' bathroom
19 Officers' heads
20 EMR, AR, AW and AEW workshop
21 Combined air technical office
22 Aircraft maintenance control office
23 Pistol shop
24 Oxyen room
25 Bomb lift
26 Cinema store
27 Unboxing space
28 Ready-use air weapons space
29 Aircraft generator room
30 Air ratings' mess
31 Seamen's mess
32 Parachute maintenance room
33 Parachute hanging room
34 Electrical ready-use store

35 Boiler room uptake
36 Hangar
37 Air weapon systems test compartment
38 Stowage for hydraulic test rig
39 Air weapons assembly space
40 Airlock
41 Store
42 Port and centre boiler room downtake
43 Light electrical workshop
44 Ready-use sonobuoy and test space
45 Aircraft instrument repair workshop
46 Battery charging room
47 Foretop part of ship locker
48 Auxiliary rise and fall lift platform
49 Hangar equipment store
50 Defective equipment sorting section

51 Mooring bay
52 Platform
53 Diving gear store
54 Barber's shop
55 Gas bottle store
56 Torpedo body room
57 Torpedo battery preparation room
58 Torpedo pistol room
59 Aircraft electrical repair shop
60 Blue Jay fire control maintenance workshop
61 Electronics maintenance workshop
62 Scanners maintenance workshop
63 Aircraft general gear workshop
64 Hydraulic and oleo workshop
65 Aircraft metal workers' workshop
66 Aircraft electrical ready-use workshop

A8/3

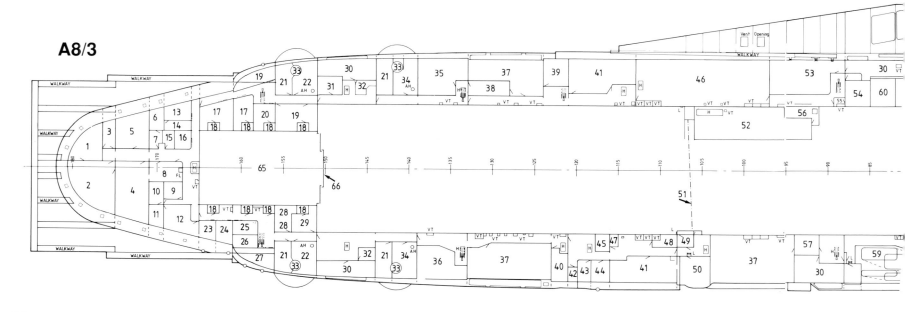

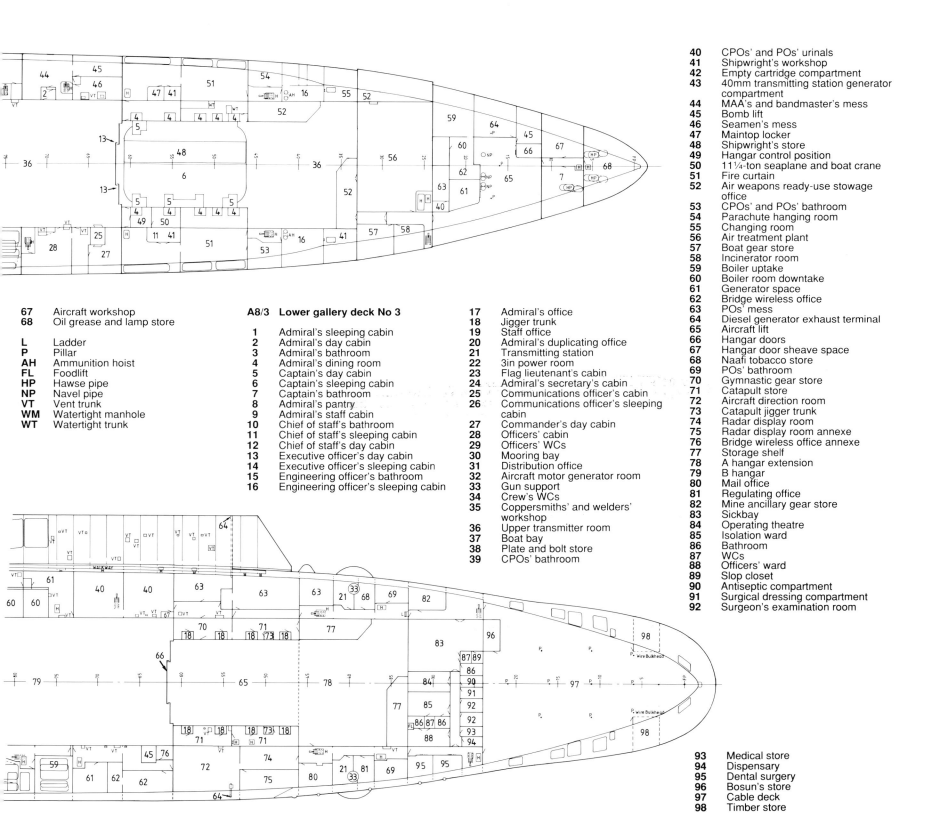

40 CPOs' and POs' urinals
41 Shipwright's workshop
42 Empty cartridge compartment
43 40mm transmitting station generator compartment
44 MAA's and bandmaster's mess
45 Bomb lift
46 Seamen's mess
47 Maintop locker
48 Shipwright's store
49 Hangar control position
50 11¼-ton seaplane and boat crane
51 Fire curtain
52 Air weapons ready-use stowage office
53 CPOs' and POs' bathroom
54 Parachute hanging room
55 Changing room
56 Air treatment plant
57 Boat gear store
58 Incinerator room
59 Boiler uptake
60 Boiler room downtake
61 Generator space
62 Bridge wireless office
63 POs' mess
64 Diesel generator exhaust terminal
65 Aircraft lift
66 Hangar doors
67 Hangar door sheave space
68 Naafi tobacco store
69 POs' bathroom
70 Gymnastic gear store
71 Catapult store
72 Aircraft direction room
73 Catapult jigger trunk
74 Radar display room
75 Radar display room annexe
76 Bridge wireless office annexe
77 Storage shelf
78 A hangar extension
79 B hangar
80 Mail office
81 Regulating office
82 Mine ancillary gear store
83 Sickbay
84 Operating theatre
85 Isolation ward
86 Bathroom
87 WCs
88 Officers' ward
89 Slop closet
90 Antiseptic compartment
91 Surgical dressing compartment
92 Surgeon's examination room

67 Aircraft workshop
68 Oil grease and lamp store

L Ladder
P Pillar
AH Ammunition hoist
FL Foodlift
HP Hawse pipe
NP Navel pipe
VT Vent trunk
WM Watertight manhole
WT Watertight trunk

A8/3 Lower gallery deck No 3

1 Admiral's sleeping cabin
2 Admiral's day cabin
3 Admiral's bathroom
4 Admiral's dining room
5 Captain's day cabin
6 Captain's sleeping cabin
7 Captain's bathroom
8 Admiral's pantry
9 Admiral's staff cabin
10 Chief of staff's bathroom
11 Chief of staff's sleeping cabin
12 Chief of staff's day cabin
13 Executive officer's day cabin
14 Executive officer's sleeping cabin
15 Engineering officer's bathroom
16 Engineering officer's sleeping cabin

17 Admiral's office
18 Jigger trunk
19 Staff office
20 Admiral's duplicating office
21 Transmitting station
22 3in power room
23 Flag lieutenant's cabin
24 Admiral's secretary's cabin
25 Communications officer's cabin
26 Communications officer's sleeping cabin
27 Commander's day cabin
28 Officers' cabin
29 Officers' WCs
30 Mooring bay
31 Distribution office
32 Aircraft motor generator room
33 Gun support
34 Crew's WCs
35 Coppersmiths' and welders' workshop
36 Upper transmitter room
37 Boat bay
38 Plate and bolt store
39 CPOs' bathroom

93 Medical store
94 Dispensary
95 Dental surgery
96 Bosun's store
97 Cable deck
98 Timber store

A General arrangement

A8/4

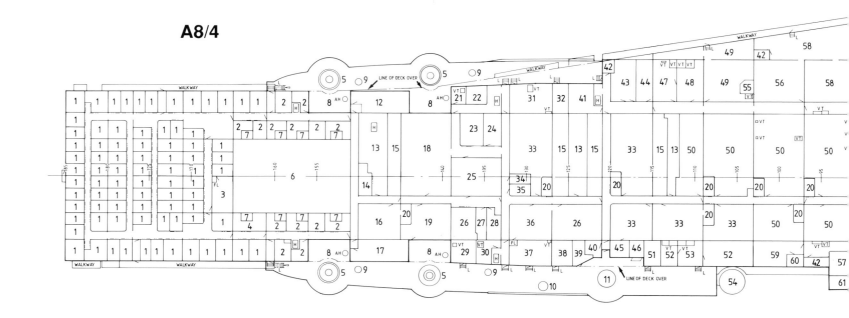

A8/4 Upper gallery deck No 2

1	Officer's cabin
2	CPOs' cabin 2 berth
3	Admiral's gallery
4	Senior officers' bathroom
5	3in/50cal mounting
6	Aircraft lift
7	Jigger trunk
8	Ready-use ammunition flat
9	MK 63 director
10	CRBF director
11	40mm Mk VI mounting
12	Officers' WCs
13	Arresting gear compartment
14	Flight deck engineer officer's office
15	Arresting gear unit
16	CPOs' and seargeants of marines' mess
17	Officers' bathroom
18	Dining hall
19	CPOs' and POs' mess
20	Pantry
21	Armament store
22	Bread pantry
23	Servery
24	Scullery
25	Ship's galley
26	Preparing room
27	Vegetable preparing room
28	Vegetable store
29	Fire control workshop
30	Ordnance store
31	Marines' store
32	Smoke store
33	CPOs' mess
34	Cool cupboard
35	Beef screen
36	Officers' galley
37	Internal combustion engine workshop
38	Type 40/60 metadyne room
39	Ready-use 40/60 magazine
40	Ready-use pyrotechnic magazine
41	CPOs' and POs' WCs
42	Aircraft motor generator compartment
43	Junior ratings' WCs
44	Bomb lift machinery
45	Bomb lift machinery compartment
46	Bomb lift
47	POs' bathroom
48	CPOs bathroom
49	Seamen's mess
50	POs' mess
51	Air weapons party store
52	Air weapons ready-use magazine
53	Jigging-up lobby
54	11¼-ton seaplane and boat crane
55	Gyro room
56	Electrical mechanics' mess
57	CPOs' and POs' canteen
58	Cooks'mess
59	Ship's electronics maintenance room
60	Store
61	Fan space
62	Boiler room downtakes
63	Briefing and ready room
64	Funnel uptakes
65	Air ratings' mess
66	Flight deck clothing store
67	Printing room
68	Developing room
69	RPOs' mess
70	Photographic office and workroom
71	Flying clothing locker space
72	Duty medical officer cabin
73	Sea staff office
74	Air chart store
75	Flying clothing store
76	Safety equipment ready-use store
77	Meteorological office
78	Strike planning room
79	Electrical equipment store
80	Air intelligence office
81	Main distribution room
82	Lift drive shaft passage
83	Officers' bridge mess
84	Admiral's sea pantry
85	Chief of staff's sea cabin
86	Double cabin
87	Chief of staff's bathroom
88	Admiral's sea cabin
89	Admiral's sea mess
90	Admiral's sea bathroom
91	Command planning room
92	Changeover switch room
93	Aircrew refreshment bar
94	Hatch cover to bomb lift machinery compartment
95	Operations room (lower level)
96	Gunnery direction room
97	GDR annexe
98	Catapult jigger trunk
99	Catapult room
100	Catapult pump room
101	Catapult workshop
102	Potato and vegetable store
103	Provision store
104	Provision issue room
105	UHF DF office
106	Victualling office
107	Marker marine store
108	Emergency conning position
109	Starboard mess and library
110	Catapult retarding pump room
111	Retardation tank

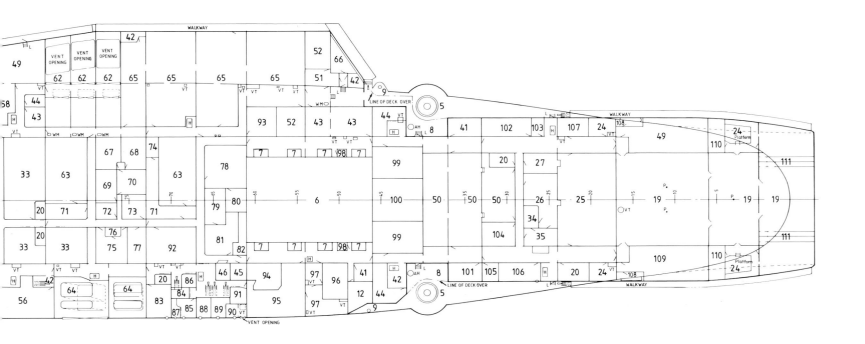

A General arrangement

A8/5

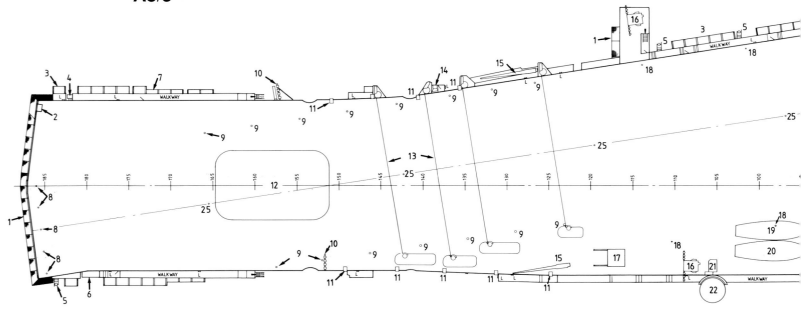

A8/5 **Flight deck No 1**

1	Hinged safety nets
2	Cover to collapsible roller fairlead
3	Double survival pack and liferaft
4	50-gallon methanol tank
5	Whip aerial
6	375-gallon methanol tank
7	Single survival pack and liferaft
8	Round-down light (white)
9	Outline light (white)
10	Hinged source light
11	Deck surface light
12	Aircraft lift
13	Arrester wire
14	Arrester gear remote control position
15	Emergency barrier mast (lowered position)
16	Deck landing mirror sight
17	Bomb lift cover
18	Contour angled deck light (red)
19	35ft medium speed motor boat
20	36ft motor pinnance
21	Instrument panel shelter

22	11¼-ton seaplane and boat crane
23	Type 963 radar office
24	Carrier controlled approach room
25	Centreline light angled deck (white)
26	Type 957 radar beacon room
27	Balloon filling station
28	Transmitter station
29	Funnel uptakes
30	Aircraft control room
31	Lobby
32	Flight deck officers' ready room
33	Aircraft handling party and ready room
34	Flight deck equipment store
35	Light aircraft crane stowage
36	Jet blast deflector
37	Deck end light (amber)
38	Axial deck contour light (red)
39	Aircraft positioner
40	Catapult control position
41	Steam catapult
42	Axial deck end light (amber)
43	Bow parking chocks
44	Axial deck centreline light (white)

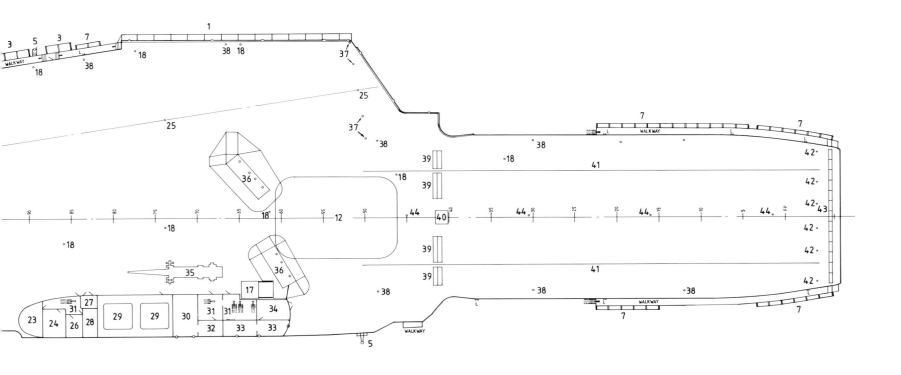

A9   SUPERSTRUCTURE DECKS

A9/1   A deck

A9/2   B deck

A9/3   C deck

A9/4   Plan above C deck

1   Ardour room
2   Lobby
3   Type 293Q radar office and LMA
4   Amplidyne room
5   No 3 W/T office
6   Funnel uptakes
7   V-UHF transmitter room
8   Double berth sea cabin
9   Bathroom
10   Admiral's bridge
11   Type 963 aerial outfit
12   Airborne early warning office
13   AEW generator room
14   Signalman's shelter
15   Visual signalling ready-use store
16   Main signal office
17   Captain's sea cabin
18   Captain's shower and WC
19   Sea cabin
20   Charthouse
21   Commander's sea cabin
22   Flying control position
23   Compass platform
24   Fan compartment
25   Type 984 LMA
26   Type 984 LMA annexe
27   Type 984 mounting machine room
28   Type 984 modulator well
29   Air plot shelter
30   MF/DF coil support
31   14ft sailing dinghy
32   Type 984 slip ring chamber

CT   Cable trunk

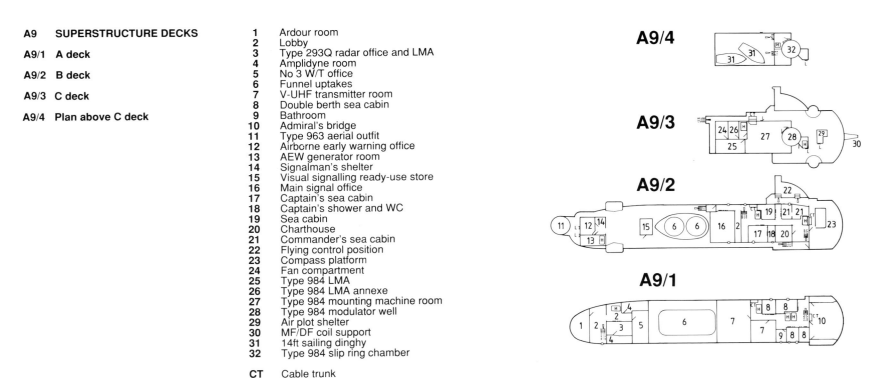

A General arrangement

**A10 EXTERNAL APPEARANCE, FROM
JUNE 1966 TO JULY 1967**

A10/1 Starboard profile

A10/2 Port profile

A10/1

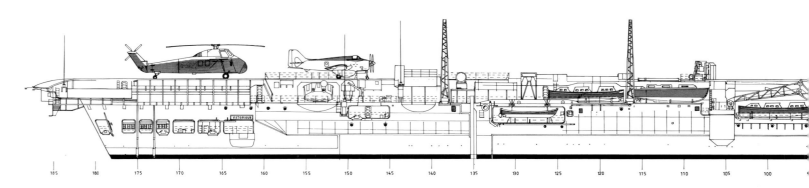

A10/2

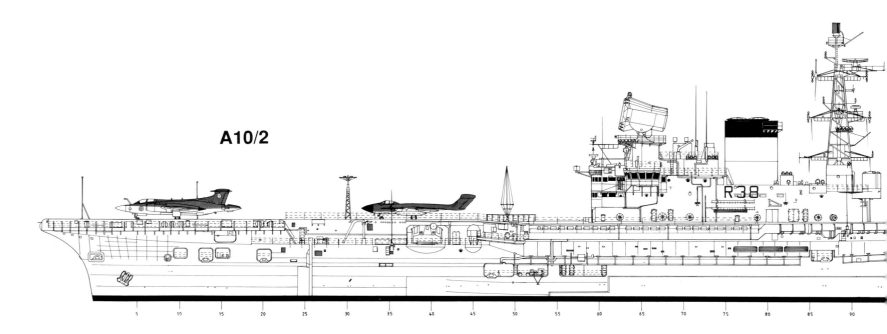

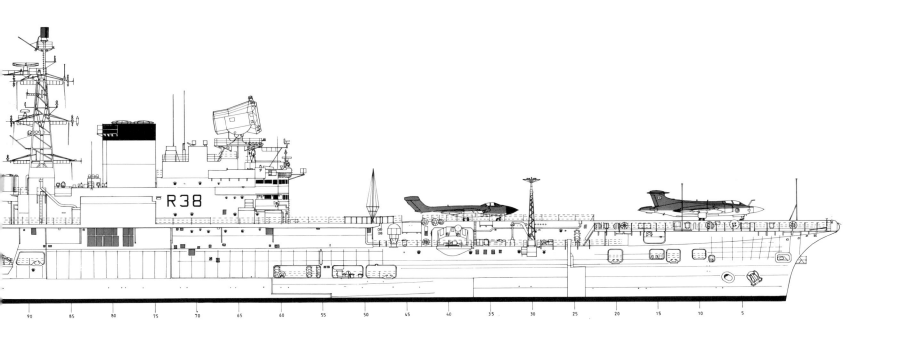

R38

90 85 80 75 70 65 60 55 50 45 40 35 30 25 20 15 10 5

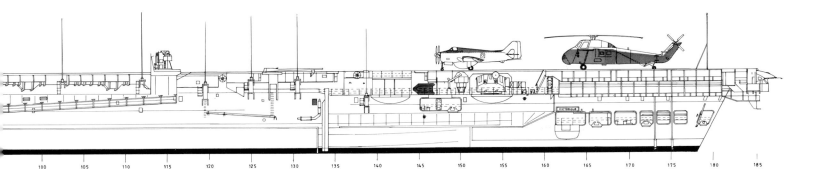

100 105 110 115 120 125 130 135 140 145 150 155 160 165 170 175 180 185

B Hull construction

B1 **LINES (1950 ONWARDS)**

B1/1 Sheer elevation (1/550 scale)

B1/2 Plan (1/550 scale)

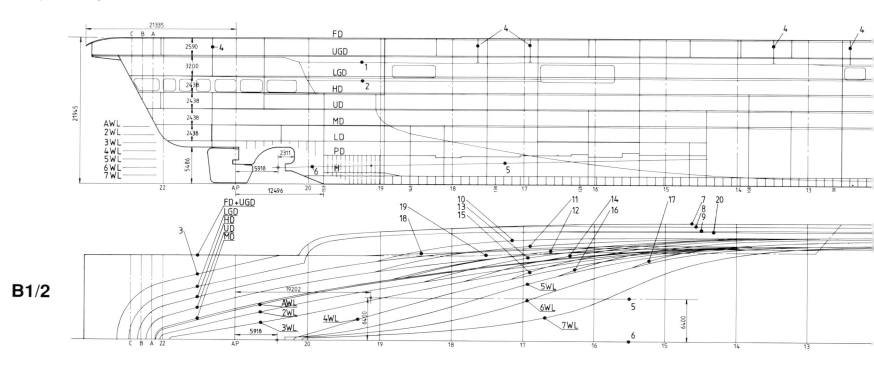

B1/1

B1/2

B2 **ARMOUR AND PROTECTIVE PLATING AS BUILT (1/1100 scale)**

B2/1 Profile

B2/2 Flight deck

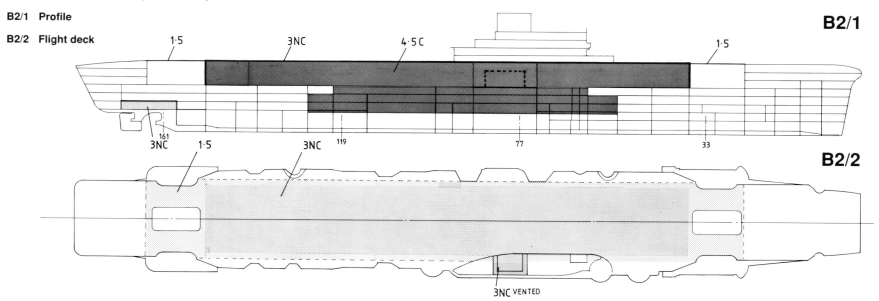

B2/1

B2/2

68

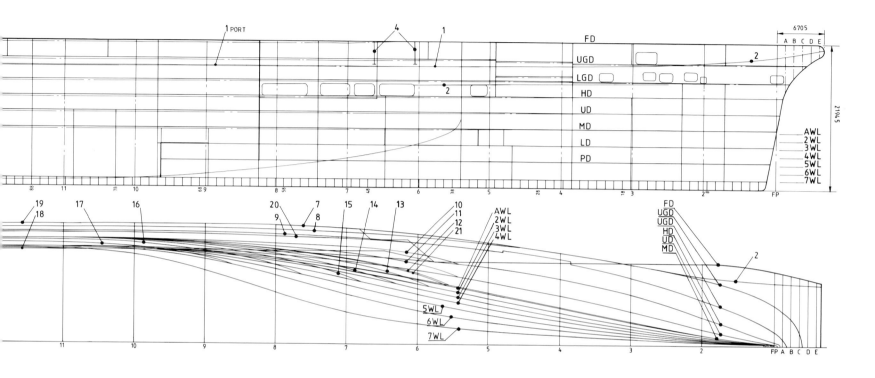

B2/3 Upper gallery deck

B2/4 Lower gallery deck

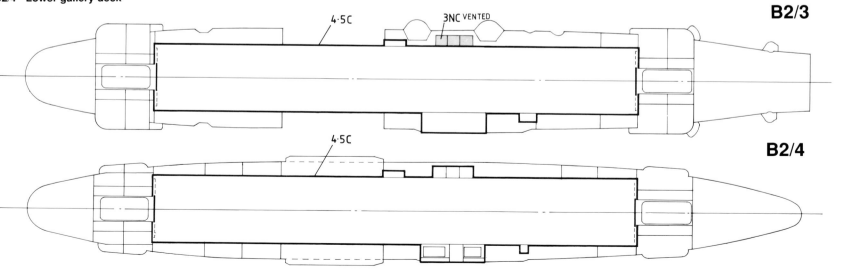

B2/3

B2/4

69

B Hull construction

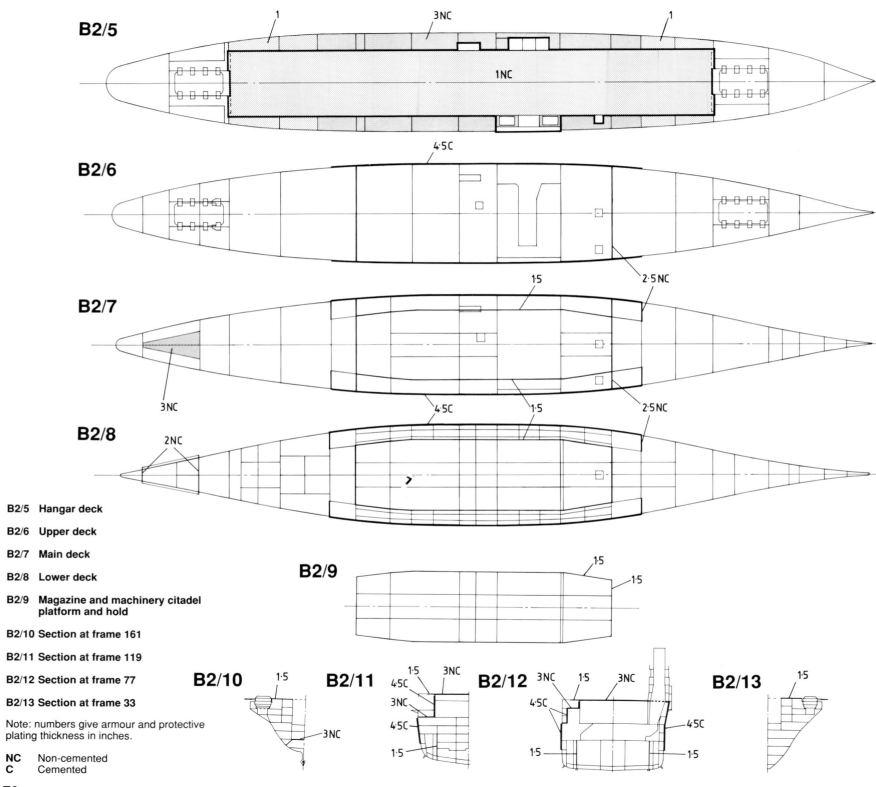

B2/5 Hangar deck

B2/6 Upper deck

B2/7 Main deck

B2/8 Lower deck

B2/9 Magazine and machinery citadel platform and hold

B2/10 Section at frame 161

B2/11 Section at frame 119

B2/12 Section at frame 77

B2/13 Section at frame 33

Note: numbers give armour and protective plating thickness in inches.

NC Non-cemented
C Cemented

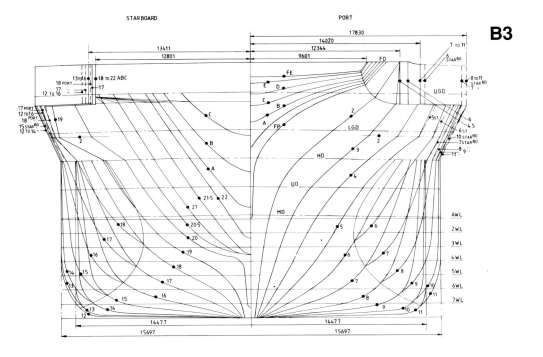

STARBOARD **PORT**

B3

B3	**Body plan (1/320 scale)**	
1	Top of gun sponson	
2	Knuckle	
3	Knuckle of upper gallery deck	
4	Beam to top of flight deck port and starboard	
5	Centreline of outer shaft	
6	Centreline of inner shaft	
7	Gun platform starboard	
8	Gun platform port	
9	Lower gallery deck starboard	
10	Bulge at hangar deck	
11	Bulge at upper deck	
12	Bulge at main deck	
13	Bulge at 2WL	
14	Bulge at 3WL	
15	Bulge at 4WL	
16	Bulge at 5WL	
17	Bulge at 6WL	
18	Flight deck port	
19	Flight deck starboard	
20	Lower gallery deck port	
21	Bulge at AWL	

FD	Flight deck
UGD	Upper gallery deck
LGD	Lower gallery deck
H	Hangar
UD	Upper deck
MD	Main deck
LD	Lower deck
PD	Platform deck
H	Hold

B4

B4 **SECTION AT FRAME 106
(LOOKING FORWARD, 1950)**

1	Walkway
2	30lb plating
3	60lb plating
4	120lb NC armour
5	60lb packing piece
6	10lb plating
7	20lb plating
8	14lb plating
9	15lb plating
10	60lb NC armour
11	40lb NC armour
12	100lb NC armour
13	80lb NC armour
14	17lb plating
15	Main longitudinal protective bulkhead 60lb 'D1'
16	Bilge keel
17	Docking keel
18	12lb plating
19	Vertical keel
20	Crane support

Note: 1 square foot of ordinary mild steel plate 1in thick weighs 40.8lb.

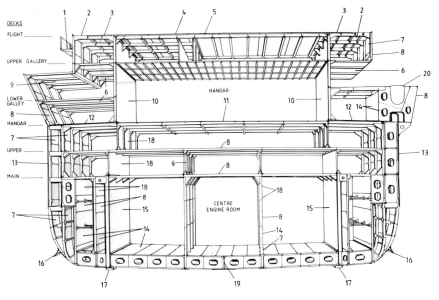

B Hull construction

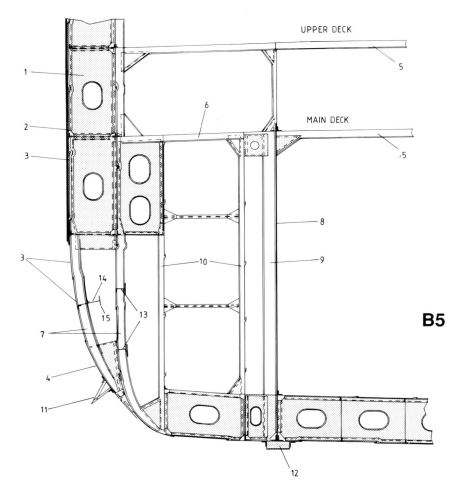

B5

B5 SECTION AT FRAME 100 IN WAY OF OIL FUEL TANKS (1/100 scale)

1   Plate frame
2   80lb NC armour
3   20lb plate
4   25lb plate
5   4in × 8in T bar beam
6   7in × 3½in L bar
7   9in × 3in × 3in channel frame
8   Main longitudinal protective bulkhead 60lb D1
9   14in × 8in × 8in I bar stiffener
10 3in × 6in T bar
11 Bilge keel
12 Docking keel
13 9in × 3in × 3in channel bar longitudinal intercostal
14 20lb DW longitudinal slotted over frames intercostal to bulkheads
15 12in × 1in rider plate

B6

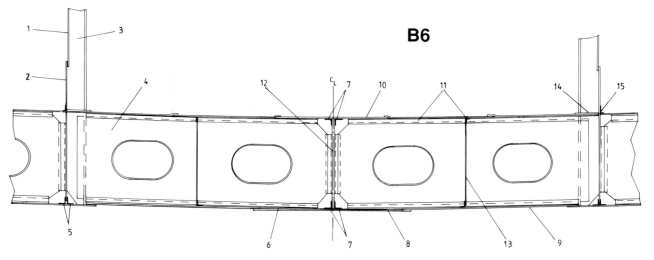

B6 SECTION THROUGH DOUBLE BOTTOM UNDER CENTRE ENGINE ROOM (1/50 scale)

1   17lb D plating
2   20lb D plating
3   5in × 10in T bar stiffener
4   14lb floor plate
5   3½in × 3½in L bar
6   Inner flat keel 35lb D plate
7   4in × 4in L bar
8   Outer flat keel plate 40lb D plate
9   Garboard strake 35lb D plate
10 Gutter strake 40lb D plate 3in × 3in L Bar
11 3in × 3in L bar
12 Vertical keel 30lb D plate
13 First longitudinal intercostal 14lb
14 Collar plate 17lb
15 3½in × 1½ L bar

72

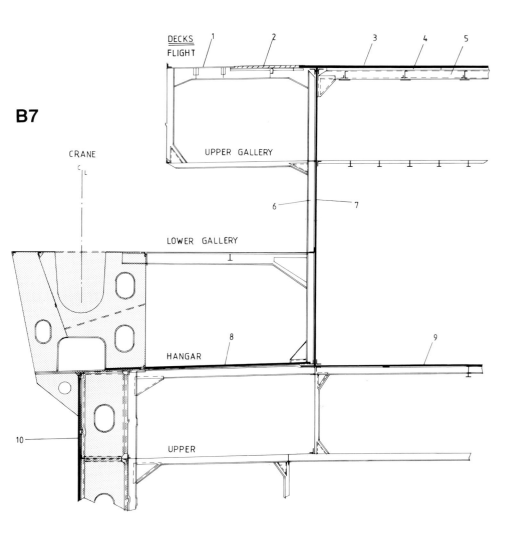

B7

CRANE
C L

UPPER GALLERY

LOWER GALLERY

HANGAR

UPPER

DECKS
FLIGHT

B7 SECTION IN WAY OF CRANE SUPPORT (1/100 scale)

1 30lb DW plate
2 60lb DW plate
3 120lb NC armour
4 60lb mild steel packing piece
5 10in × 3½in × 3½in channel beam intercostal
6 8in × 6in × 6in I bar sitffener
7 60lb NC armour
8 100lb NC armour
9 40lb NC armour
10 80lb NC armour

B8 SECTION AT FRAME 16 LOOKING FORWARD (1/200 scale)

1 20lb DW plate
2 4in × 8in T bar girder
3 4in × 8in T bar beam
4 12in × 6in × 6in I bar girder
5 4in × 8in T bar stiffener
6 6in × 12in T bar girder
7 3½in × 7in T bar beam
8 14lb plating
9 12lb plating
10 10lb plating
11 6in × 10in T bar
12 4in × 8in T bar intercostal
13 3½in × 7in T bar intercostal
14 4in × 8in T bar intercostal
15 3in × 6in T beam
16 14lb floor plate

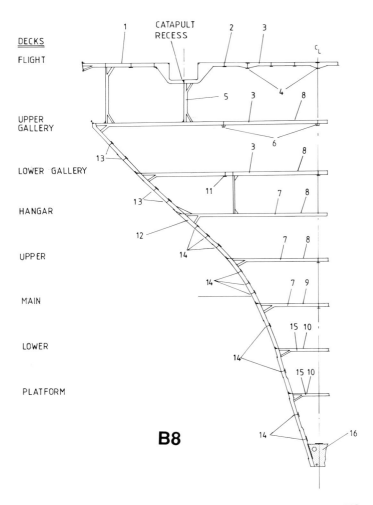

DECKS
FLIGHT

CATAPULT RECESS

C L

UPPER GALLERY

LOWER GALLERY

HANGAR

UPPER

MAIN

LOWER

PLATFORM

B8

B9

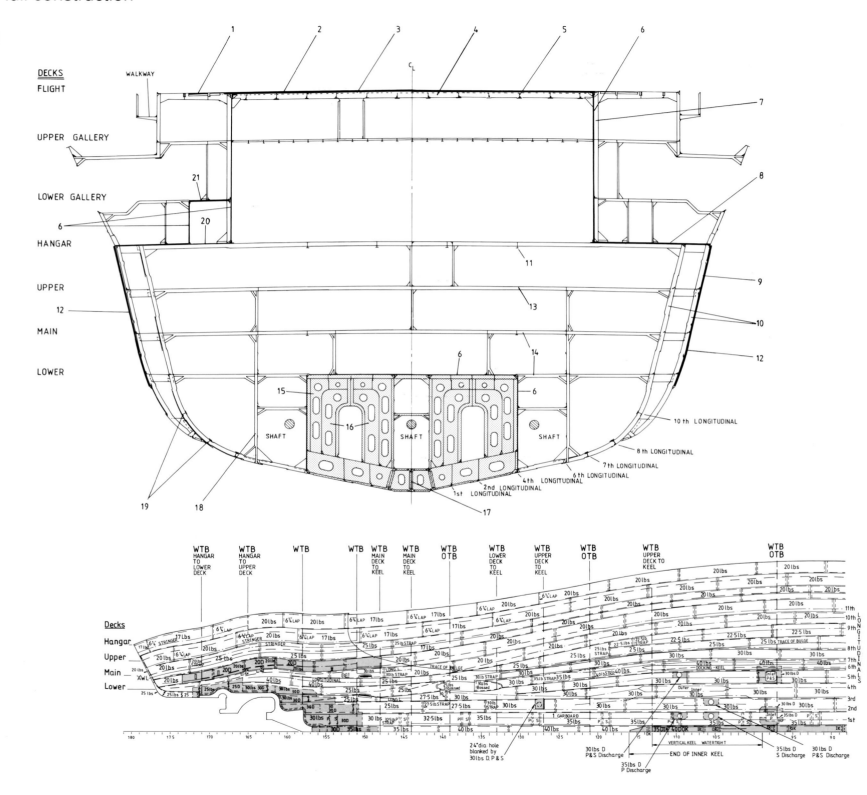

B9 SECTION AT FRAME 124 LOOKING AFT (1/200 scale)

1. 60lb 'DW' armour
2. 120lb NC armour
3. 60lb mild steel packing piece 3½in wide
4. 10in × 3½in × 3½in channel beam intercostal
5. 10in × 3½in × 3½in channel girder continuous
6. 60lb NC armour
7. 8in × 6in × 6in I bar stiffener
8. 100lb NC armour
9. 20lb plating behind armour
10. 9in × 3in × 3in channel bar frame
11. 12in × 6in × 6in I bar girder
12. 80lb NC armour
13. 4in × 8in T bar
14. 3½in × 7in T bar
15. Outer diaphragm plate
16. Inner diaphragm plate
17. Vertical keel
18. 3in × 6in T bar stiffener
19. 9in × 3in × 3in channel longitudinal intercostal
20. 40lb NC armour
21. 120lb NC armour

B10

DECKS
FLIGHT
JIGGER TRUNK
LIFT
UPPER GALLERY
LOWER GALLERY
HANGAR
UPPER
MAIN
LOWER

B10 SECTION IN WAY OF 3in MK 6 MOUNTING AT FRAME 153 (1/200 scale)

1. 30lb DW plate
2. 60lb DW plate
3. 120lb NC armour
4. 3½in × 7in T bar stiffener
5. 4in × 8in T bar stiffener
6. 3in × 6in T bar stiffener
7. 3in × 6in T bar beam
8. 4in × 8in T bar beam
9. 9in × 3in × 3in channel bar frame
10. 4in × 8in T bar frame
11. 9in × 3in × 3in longitudinal channel
12. 60lb NC armour

B11 EXPANSION OF OUTER BOTTOM PLATING FROM KEEL TO HANGAR DECK STARBOARD SIDE 1950 (1/600 scale)

Note: port side similar except where indicated. Straps correspond to the weight of plating joined; for example, two 20lb plates would have a 20lb strap. All straps were triple riveted. Plate doubling is indicated by shaded areas.

BW	Butt weld
D	Doubling
DIK	Double inner keel
DOK	Double outer keel
HP	Hawse pipe
P	Port
S	Starboard

B11

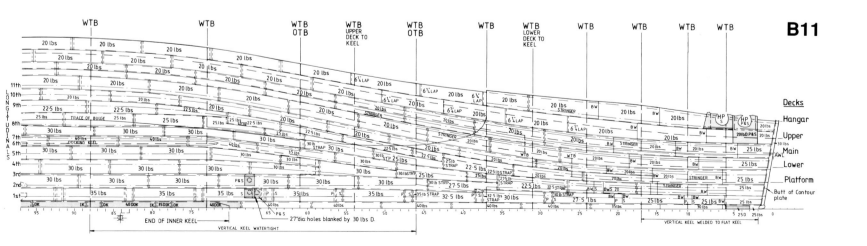

C Machinery

C1/1

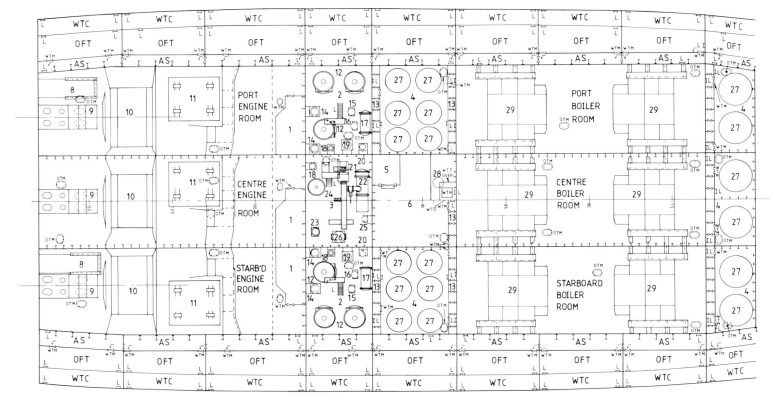

Γ W.T. Manholes into W.T. Compartment under Oil Fuel Tanks

C1	**GENERAL ARRANGEMENTS OF MACHINERY AS BUILT** (1/275 scale)				

1	Overflow feed tank	20	Overflow tank pump	39	Air ejectors
2	Evaporating machinery compartment	21	LP air compressor	40	Main feed tank
3	After LP compressor room	22	Feed heater	41	Renovated oil tank
4	Petrol tank compartment	23	Hangar spraying pump	42	Steering gear
5	Bomb lift	24	Air reservoir	43	Boiler room
6	No 1 warhead room	25	Feed heater drain pump	44	Boiler uptake
7	150-ton pump room	26	Oil fuel transfer pump	45	Forced draft fan
8	Turbo generator seating	27	Petrol tank	46	Escape hatch
9	Thrust block seating	28	150-ton pump	47	Boiler room vent and forced draft fan inlet (over)
10	Gear case seating	29	Boiler seating	48	No 2 warhead and No 5 bomb room
11	Condenser seating	30	Turbo-generator	49	Auxiliary boiler room vent
12	Evaporator	31	Torpedo exhaust fan	50	Air lock
13	Reserve feed tank	32	Torpedo supply fan	51	Distiller
14	Distillery pump	33	Turning gear	52	Telephone exchange
15	Feed heater drain pump	34	Oil coolers	53	Machinery control room
16	De-aerator extraction pump	35	Gear case	54	Deck
17	Drain cooler	36	LP turbine	55	Control panel
18	Fire and bilge pump	37	HP turbine	56	Cupboard
19	Drain and cooler pump	38	Silent cabinet		

C1/1 Plan of engine and boiler rooms at hold deck level

C1/2 Plan of engine and boiler rooms at platform deck level

C1/2

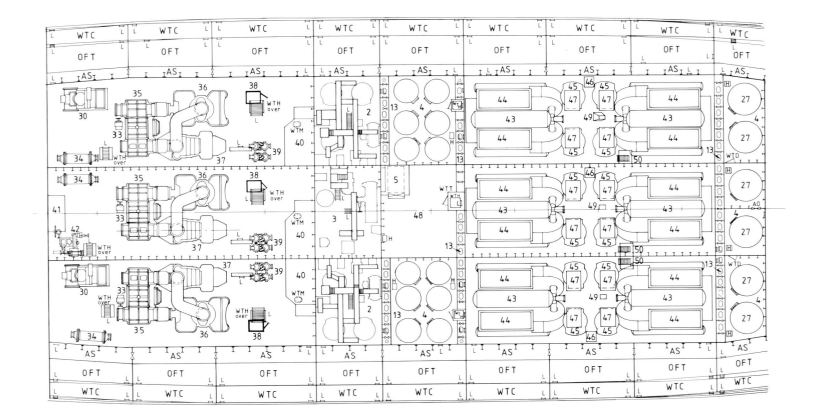

57	Steam pipe passage	76	Lub oil tank	95	Main circulating pump	**AO**	Access opening
58	Bin	77	Electric lead passage	96	Closed feed control valve	**AS**	Air space
59	Dwarf bulkhead	78	Oil fuel working space	97	Discharge outlet	**F**	Floor
60	Stowage (over)	79	Lobby	98	Water extraction pump	**H**	Hatch
61	Auxiliary boiler room fan	80	Lolos strainer	99	Forced lubrication pump	**L**	Ladder
62	Hot water storage tank	81	Compressor	100	Drying room	**OFT**	Oil fuel tank
63	Exhaust fan	82	HP air compressor	101	Firebrick store	**OTB**	Oil-tight bulkhead
64	Turbo generator room	83	Reservoir	102	Stokers' dressing room	**OTM**	Oil-tight manhole
65	Supply fan	84	LP air compressor	103	HA calculating position	**WTB**	Watertight bulkhead
66	Switch gear	85	Air receiver	104	Switchboard room	**WTC**	Watertight compartment
67	Saveall	86	Soot plant	105	Oil fuel service pump	**WTD**	Watertight door
68	Valve chest	87	Motor	106	Supplementary oil fuel pump	**WTH**	Watertight hatch
69	Petrol control compartment	88	Furnace	107	Funnel uptake	**WTM**	Watertight manhole
70	Depth gauge	89	W/T power supply	108	Incinerator funnel	**WTT**	Watertight trunk
71	Petrol pump	90	Condenser	109	Galley funnel		
72	Filter	91	FL oil filters	110	Boiler room vent cover		
73	Bench	92	Pom-pom magazine	111	Boiler room vent opening		
74	Rotary oil pump	93	No 4 bomb room				
75	Aircraft lubricating oil store	94	De-aerator				

C Machinery

C1/3 Plan of engine and boiler rooms at lower deck level

C1/4 Longitudinal section of engine rooms

See key pages 76–7

C1/3

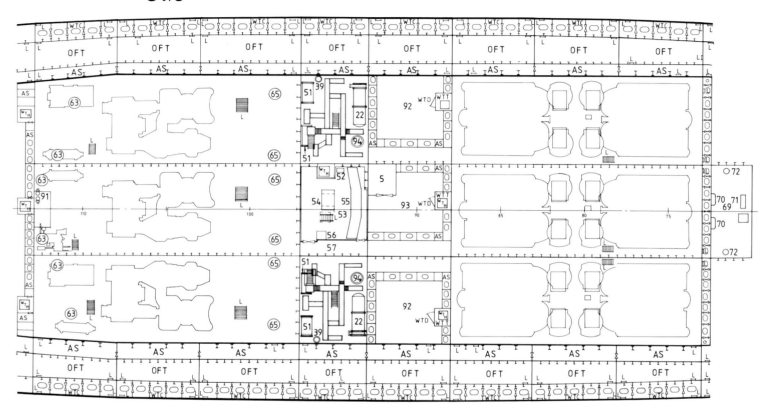

C1/4

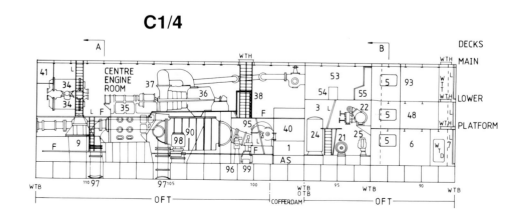

See key pages 76–77

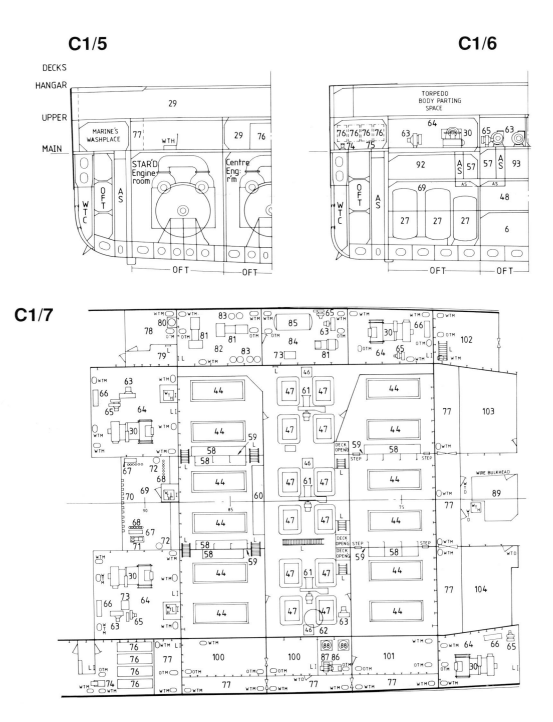

C1/8

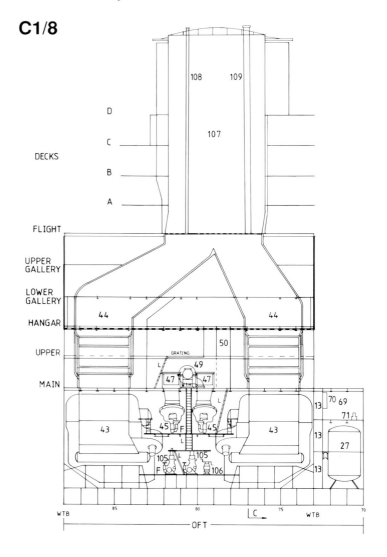

C1/9

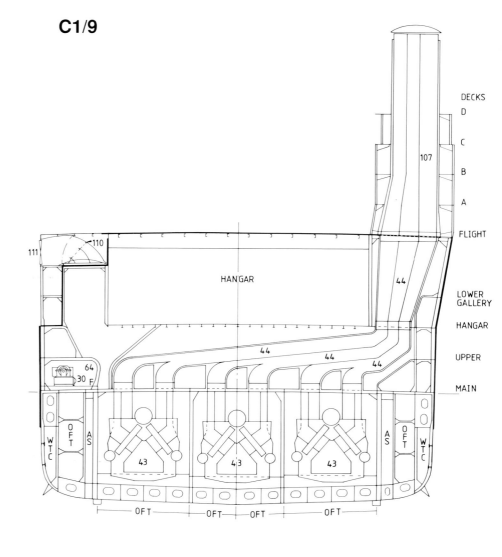

C1/8 Longitudinal section of boiler rooms

C1/9 Section at 'C' looking forward

See key pages 76–7

C2	CUTAWAY OF ADMIRALTY THREE-DRUM BOILER
C3	LOW PRESSURE TURBINE
C4	EXPLODED VIEW OF HIGH PRESSURE TURBINE
C5	MAIN CONDENSER
C6	MAIN GEAR CASE

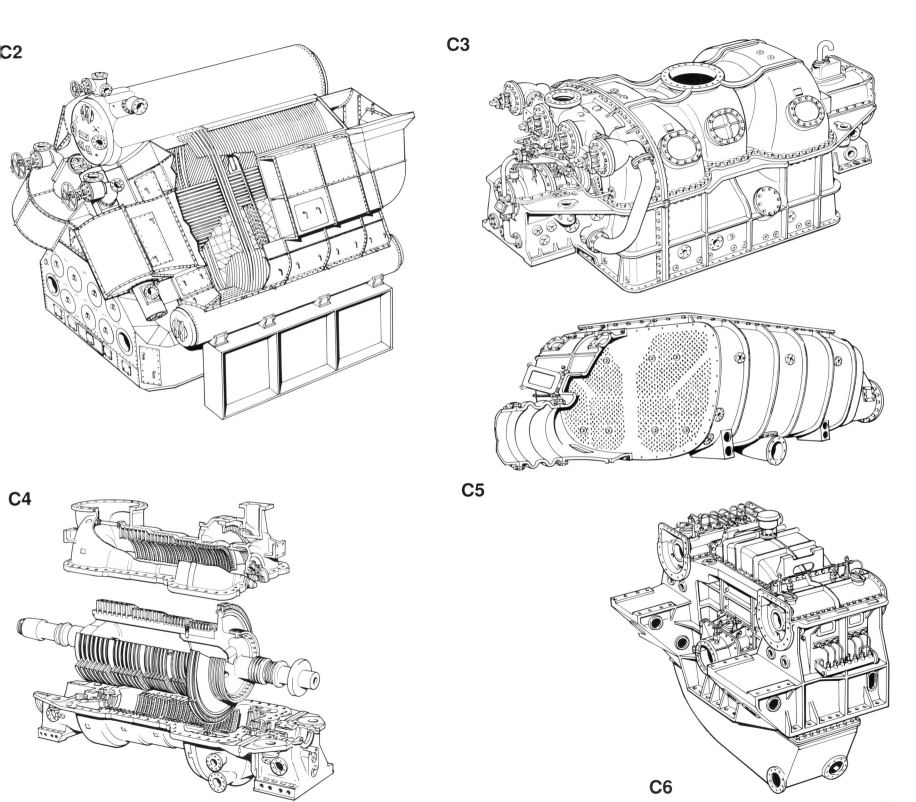

C2

C3

C4

C5

C6

C Machinery

**C7   PROPELLER AND STEERING
GEAR ARRANGEMENTS**
(1/275 scale)

C7/1   Plan of propeller shafts at hold
deck

C7/2   Longitudinal section

C7/3   Sections looking aft

C7/4   Plan of steering gear compartment

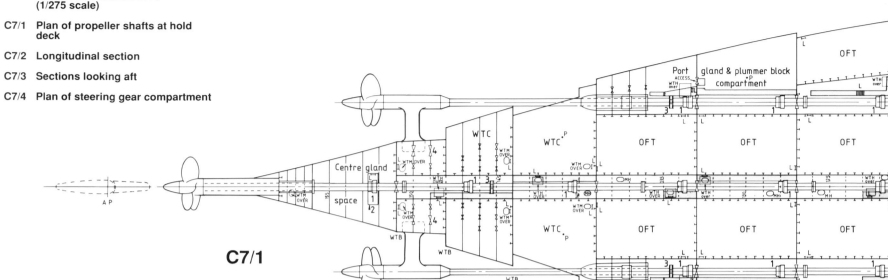

C7/1

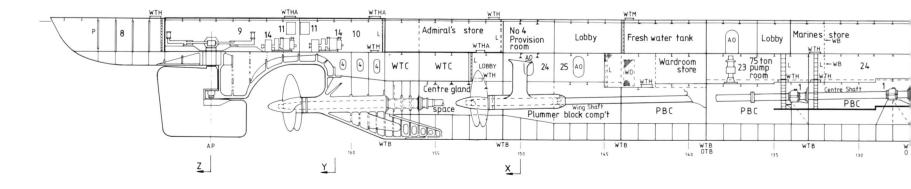

C7/2

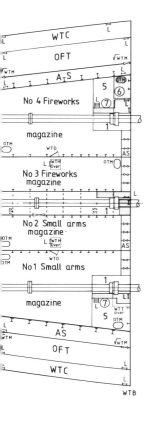

1	Plummer block
2	Portable plate
3	Friction block
4	Lightening holes
5	150-ton pump room and plummer block compartment
6	Hangar spray pump platform
7	150-ton pump
8	Officers' baggage room
9	Tiller flat
10	Steering gear store
11	Oil replenishment tank
12	Mechanical control pedestal
13	Silent cabinet
14	Variable delivery pump
15	Knuckle line of armour (over)
16	Steel shelf
17	Cupboard with drawers under
18	Steel bench
19	Starter motor
20	Knuckle
21	Line of bulkhead
22	Bulkhead (over)
23	75-ton hull and fire pump
24	Engineers' spare gear store
25	Wardroom wine store

MH	Manhole
NWTM	Non watertight manhole
PBC	Plummer block compartment
WB	Wire bulkhead
WD	Wire door
WTHA	Watertight hatch armoured

C7/3

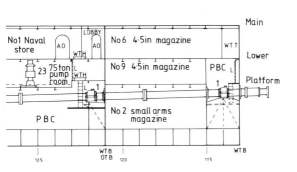

C7/4

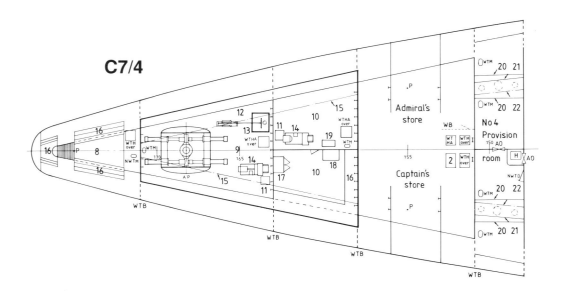

C Machinery

C8   MAIN THRUST BLOCK

C8/1   Sectioned side elevation (no scale)

C8/2   Front elevation (no scale)

C8/3   Cutaway view

C9   MITCHELL PLUMMER BLOCK

C10   SHAFT LOCKING GEAR

C11   EVAPORATOR SHELL AND MOUNTINGS

C12   FOSTER WHEELER BOILER (fitted during modernisation)

C8/1

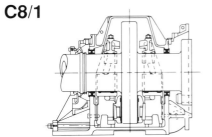

C8/2

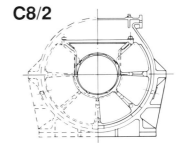

C8/3

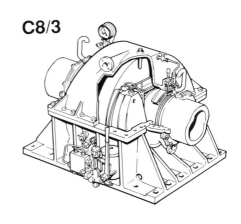

C9

C10

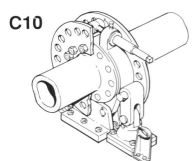

C11

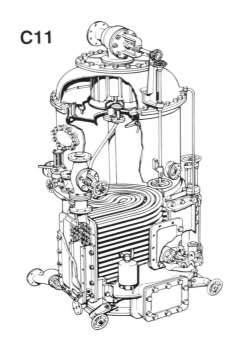

C12

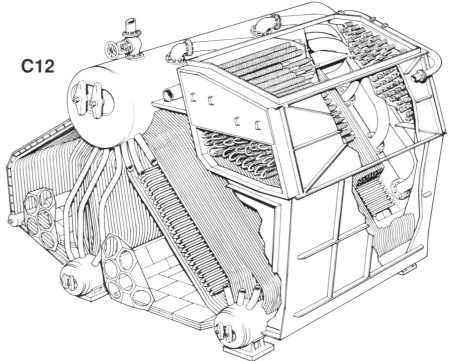

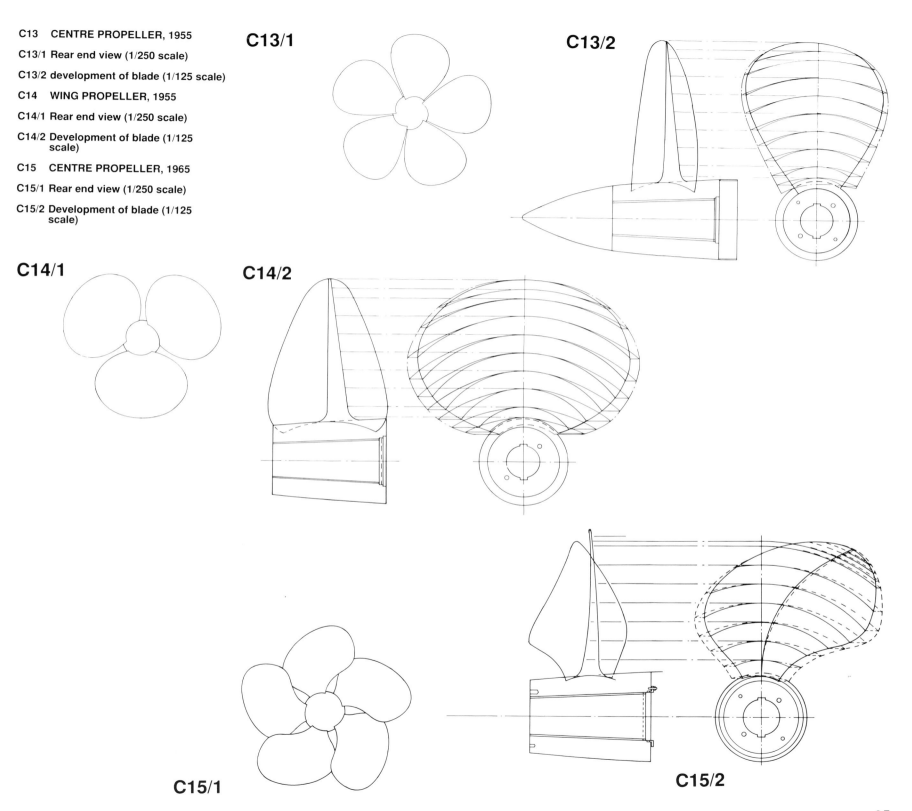

C13   CENTRE PROPELLER, 1955

C13/1 Rear end view (1/250 scale)

C13/2 development of blade (1/125 scale)

C14   WING PROPELLER, 1955

C14/1 Rear end view (1/250 scale)

C14/2 Development of blade (1/125 scale)

C15   CENTRE PROPELLER, 1965

C15/1 Rear end view (1/250 scale)

C15/2 Development of blade (1/125 scale)

C13/1

C13/2

C14/1

C14/2

C15/1

C15/2

D Accommodation

D1   **ADMIRAL'S AND CAPTAIN'S ACCOMMODATION ON THE LOWER DECK, AS FITTED (1/300 scale)**

1   Admiral's sleeping cabin
2   Counter top
3   Chest of drawers
4   Dressing table
5   Heater
6   Wardrobe
7   Bedstead (drawers under)
8   Shelf
9   Bath
10   Admiral's bathroom
11   Folding seat
12   Cabinet
13   Folding table
14   Admiral's spare cabin
15   Two beds
16   Two lockers
17   WC
18   Admiral's day cabin
19   Knee-hole table
20   Fan (over)
21   Cupboard and drawers
22   Settee
23   Table
24   Electric fire
25   Curtain
26   Sideboard
27   Drawers and cupboard under counter top
28   Admiral's dining cabin or officers' sleeping quarters
29   Captain's day cabin
30   Loudspeaker
31   Roll top desk
32   Bookcase
33   Leaf locker
34   Captain's sleeping cabin
35   Captain's bathroom
36   Lobby
37   Confidential books
38   First aid cabinet
39   Cinema projector room
40   Projector
41   Receiver
42   Rewind room
43   Admiral's pantry
44   Food lift
45   Exhaust fan
46   Toaster
47   Electric hot cupboard
48   Fridge
49   Plate rack (over)
50   Sink

D2   **WARDROOM AND ANTE-ROOM ON UPPER DECK, AS FITTED (1/300 scale)**

1   Wardroom ante-room
2   Electric fire
3   Newspaper rack
4   Supply fan
5   Fan (over)
6   Curtain
7   Card table
8   Knee-hole table
9   Bookcase
10   Atlas and chart box
11   Gateleg table
12   Hydraulic tank
13   Fire and repair cupboard
14   Reel (over)
15   Wardroom
16   Loudspeaker
17   Rack
18   Radiator
19   Cupboard
20   Stool and piano
21   Serving hatch counter
22   Letter-rack
23   Napkin rack
24   Carving table
25   Table
26   Sideboard
27   Ammunition conveyor
28   Wardroom wine pantry
29   Tumbler rack (over)
30   Dresser
31   Wine glass rack (over)
32   Glass washer
33   Wine bin
34   Hinged seat
35   Sink
36   Wardroom pantry
37   Stainless steel dresser with drawers
38   Food lift
39   Plate rack
40   Egg rack
41   Hot cupboard
42   Refrigerator
43   Scullery
44   Warrant officers' mess
45   Warrant officers' rest room
46   Warrant officers' pantry
47   Motor dynamo
48   Timber stowage
49   Exhaust fan
50   Regulator for DG motors
51   Stowage for door ramp
52   Commander's office
53   FAA office
54   Captain's office
55   Engineer's office
56   Ledgers
57   Writing table
58   Locker
59   Wash basin
60   Bed
61   Shelf
62   Pack rack
63   Steel cabinet
64   Drawing table

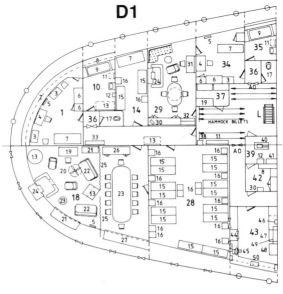

D1

D2

D3   **JUNIOR RATES' MESS BETWEEN FRAMES 37 AND 46 ON THE UPPER DECK, AS FITTED** (1/300 scale)

1. Mess rack (over)
2. Two kit lockers
3. Three kit lockers
4. Seat
5. Table
6. Hammock stowage
7. Supply fan
8. Cleaning locker
9. Electric hot cupboard
10. Reel

D4   **JUNIOR RATES' MESS BETWEEN FRAMES 37 AND 46 ON THE UPPER DECK, AFTER 1963** (1/300 scale)

1. One kit locker
2. Two kit lockers
3. Three kit lockers
4. Two-tier bunks
5. Three-tier bunks
6. Greatcoat locker
7. No 1 USB and DC base
8. Damage control locker
9. Ammunition hoist
10. Table
11. Bollard hoist
12. Control panel
13. Battery holder

L   Ladder
P   Pillar
M   Manhole
WTD   Watertight door
WTH   Watertight hatch

D3

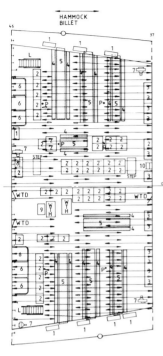

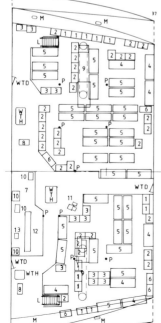

D4

D5 TYPICAL MESS TABLE AS FITTED

D5/1   Profile

D5/2   Plan

1. Hook
2. Leg stowed
3. Clip
4. Stay
5. Plate feet
6. Seat (spruce)
7. Table (spruce)
8. Rim (Borneo wood)

D6   **THREE-TIER BUNK, FITTED AFTER MODERNISATION**

1. Boot drawer
2. Suitcase stowage
3. Bedding drawer
4. Bunk light

D5/1

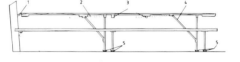

D5/2

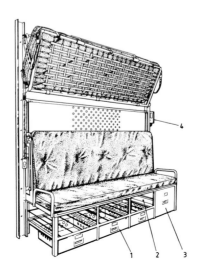

D6

E1/1

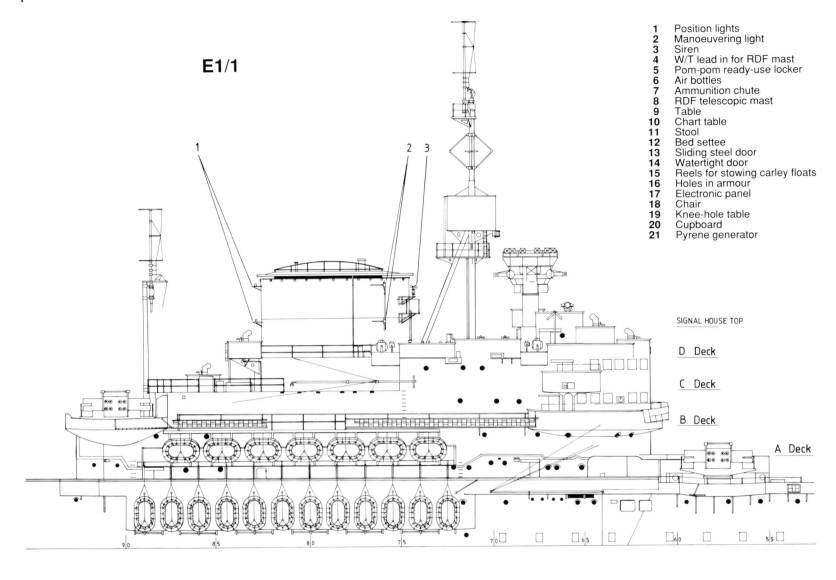

1	Position lights
2	Manoeuvering light
3	Siren
4	W/T lead in for RDF mast
5	Pom-pom ready-use locker
6	Air bottles
7	Ammunition chute
8	RDF telescopic mast
9	Table
10	Chart table
11	Stool
12	Bed settee
13	Sliding steel door
14	Watertight door
15	Reels for stowing carley floats
16	Holes in armour
17	Electronic panel
18	Chair
19	Knee-hole table
20	Cupboard
21	Pyrene generator

SIGNAL HOUSE TOP

D Deck

C Deck

B Deck

A Deck

E1 ISLAND SUPERSTRUCTURE, BRIDGE, NAVIGATION AND CONTROL POSITIONS, AS FITTED (1/250 scale)

E1/1 Starboard profile

22	Pyrene cylinders
23	Bath
24	Folding seat
25	Wash basin
26	Hot water tank
27	Locker for aero engine starters
28	Telephone board
29	Flight deck and signal light switchboard
30	Crash barrier control panel
31	Wardrobe
32	Telephone junction box
33	Bomb lift cage
34	Book shelf
35	Steel helmet bin
36	Flame float locker

37 Step
38 Loading platform
39 Sounding machine
40 Hinged portable boom
41 Sounding boom
42 Sounding gear locker
43 2pdr pom-pom mounting
44 Carrier identification group lights
45 Bomb lift watertight door
46 Steel doors
47 Stowage for pom-pom boxes
48 Vent outlets with cover plate (over)
49 Signal group light (red, white and green)
50 Oil fuel tank
51 Settee
52 Stowage for charts
53 Mast
54 Plotting table
55 Pilot lamp box for aircraft signal lights
56 Aldis resistance and stowage box
57 Screen bulkhead
58 Box for masthead and port yardarm flashing keys
59 Indicator lamp and key for manoeuvering lights
60 Captain's sight
61 Gyro compass azimuth repeater
62 Kent clear view screen
63 Pelorus
64 Wind deflector
65 Wind baffles
66 Standard compass
67 Kit locker
68 Seat
69 Supply fan
70 Sliding blackboard
71 Pneumatic tube pump and motor
72 Bunks
73 Desk
74 Engine room telegraph and revolution telegraph
75 Steering pedestal with dual telemotor transmitters
76 Carley floats
77 Pom-pom director
78 Affirmative signalling shutter
79 Aircraft signal flag locker
80 Fire control junction box
81 Conning bridge
82 Aircraft signalling boom
83 Fresh water tank
84 Mast strut
85 Ready-use signal store
86 Rack
87 Bow light box
88 Locker for signal books
89 Box for signalling keys
90 Box for steam signal cones
91 20in signalling projector
92 10in signalling projector
93 NUC locker (not under command)
94 Signal flag locker
95 Hooded table
96 Air lookout
97 Air defence officer's and star shell sight
98 Searchlight sight
99 Semaphore
100 Support for telescope
101 Tactical and navigation rangefinder
102 DF sence aerials
103 Funnels for answering pendants

E1/2 Signal house top

E1/3 D deck

E1/4 C deck

E1/5 B deck

E1/2

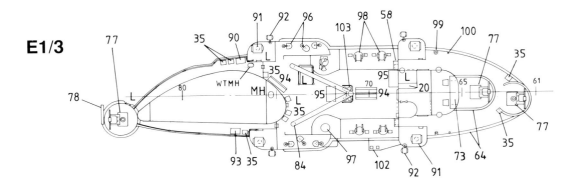

E1/3

E1/4

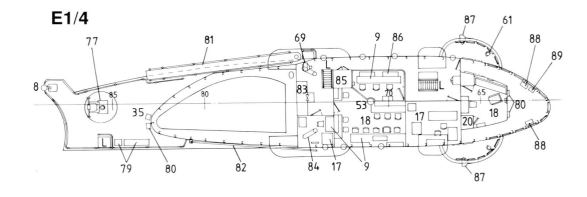

E1/5

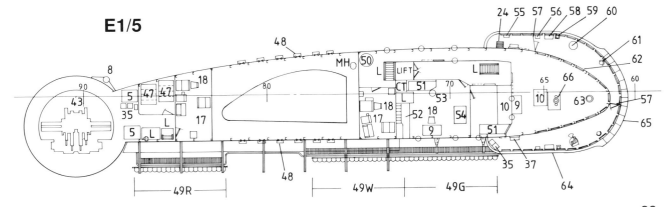

E Superstructure

E1/6   **A deck**

E1/7   **Flight deck**

E1/8   **Port profile**

See key on pages 88–9

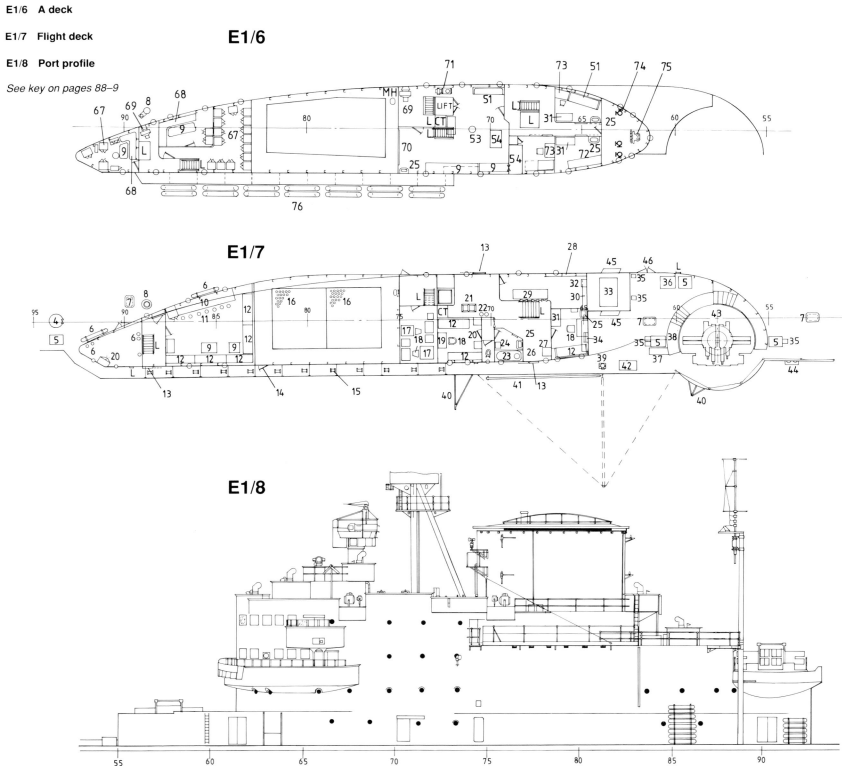

E1/6

E1/7

E1/8

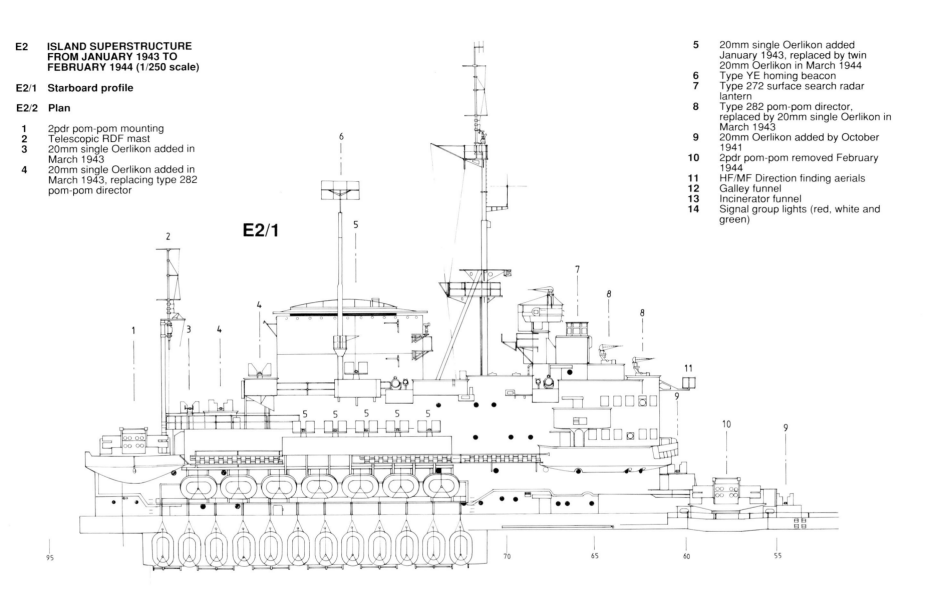

E2 ISLAND SUPERSTRUCTURE FROM JANUARY 1943 TO FEBRUARY 1944 (1/250 scale)

E2/1 Starboard profile

E2/2 Plan

1 2pdr pom-pom mounting
2 Telescopic RDF mast
3 20mm single Oerlikon added in March 1943
4 20mm single Oerlikon added in March 1943, replacing type 282 pom-pom director

5 20mm single Oerlikon added January 1943, replaced by twin 20mm Oerlikon in March 1944
6 Type YE homing beacon
7 Type 272 surface search radar lantern
8 Type 282 pom-pom director, replaced by 20mm single Oerlikon in March 1943
9 20mm Oerlikon added by October 1941
10 2pdr pom-pom removed February 1944
11 HF/MF Direction finding aerials
12 Galley funnel
13 Incinerator funnel
14 Signal group lights (red, white and green)

E2/1

E2/2

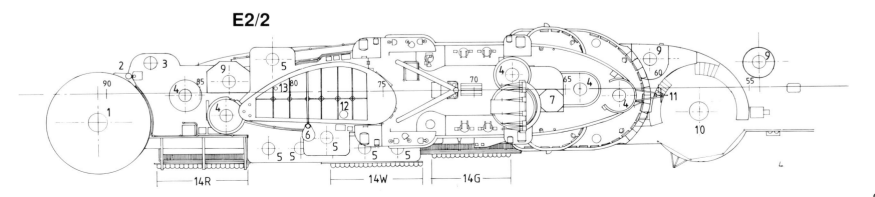

E2/3 Port profile

See key on page 91

E2/3

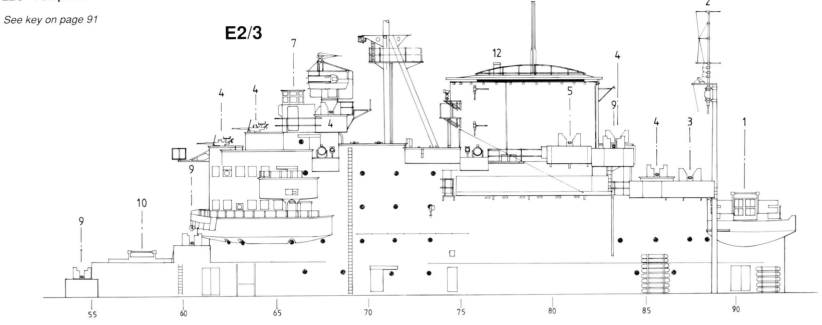

E3 ISLAND SUPERSTRUCTURE 1958
(1/250 scale)

E3/1 Starboard profile

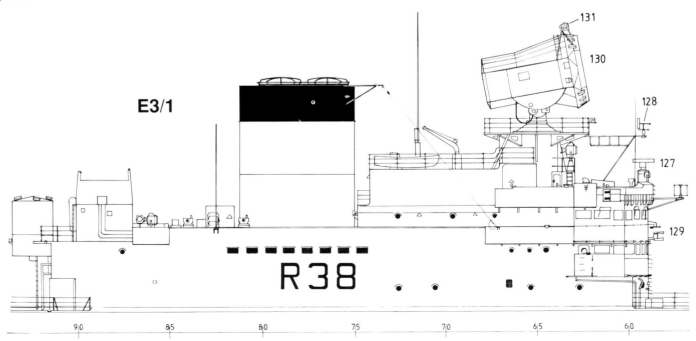

E3/1

R38

1 Deck broadcast
2 Hydrogen bottle stowage
3 Foam locker
4 Type 963 office
5 Transmitter
6 Cabinet
7 Bench
8 Resolver outfit
9 Reels for aircraft servicing cables
10 Aircraft electric servicing position
11 Hinged desk
12 Viewing unit
13 Carrier controlled approach room
14 Control unit
15 Radio beacon room
16 Lobby
17 Loudspeaker
18 Computer cabinet
19 Aerial control unit
20 Balloon filling station
21 Cupboard
22 CCA transmitter room
23 Contour light axial deck (red)
24 Funnel uptake
25 Bomb transfer davit
26 Obstruction light
27 Aircraft fuelling position (Avcat)
28 Stowage position for stump masts
29 Bow window
30 Aircraft control room
31 Raised platform
32 Aircraft serviceability board
33 Telephone control box
34 Flight deck lighting switchboard
35 Radiator
36 Hatch
37 Flight deck officers' ready room
38 Bed settee
39 Desk
40 Aircraft handling and party ready room
41 Flight deck equipment store
42 Stowage for fire-fighting suits
43 Rack
44 Locker
45 Screen
46 Bomb lift cover
47 Ardour room
48 Power supply unit
49 Supply vent
50 Type 293Q office and LMA
51 Amplidyne room
52 Motor generator
53 Air-conditioning unit
54 Electronic warfare office
55 Amplifier
56 V-UHF transmitter room
57 UHF receiver room
58 Exhaust vent
59 Double berth sea cabin
60 Officers' bridge bathroom
61 Azimuth repeater
62 Signal flashing keys
63 High chair
64 Open bridge
65 Admiral's bridge
66 Display radar
67 Curtain
68 WC
69 Power unit for type 974 radar
70 Two beds
71 Type 963 aerial support
72 Aerial insulator
73 Airborne early warning office
74 Signalman's shelter
75 Crashlanding floodlight (red)
76 Stowage for NUC balls (not under command)
77 Funnel for answering pendant
78 10in signalling projector
79 20in signalling projector
80 Flag locker
81 Lantern stowage box
82 Saluting gun
83 Vent fan
84 Visual signalling ready-use store
85 Emergency whip aerial
86 Ammunition locker
87 Main signal TP room
88 Captain's sea cabin
89 Sea cabin
90 Charthouse
91 Speed flag socket
92 Bed settee
93 Chart table
94 Box for flashing keys
95 Key for daylight signalling lantern
96 Communicator's hooded desk
97 Weatherproof light
98 Pelorus
99 Flying control position
100 Gyro compass repeater
101 Compass platform
102 Tactical display
103 Turbo blower and fan compartment
104 Type 984 LMA
105 Air lookout sight
106 Type 984 mounting machine room
107 Lubrication supply vent
108 Verifying sight
109 Airplot shelter
110 Gunnery direction officer's sight
111 Loudhailer
112 Whip aerial
113 Sight selector switch
114 MF/DF frame coil
115 Type 984 modulator well
116 Bowlight
117 Scupper
118 Winch
119 Hinged davit
120 14ft sailing dinghy
121 Type 984 slip ring
122 Ship's crest
123 Magnetic broadcast loop
124 Navigation siren
125 D/F sense aerial
126 QM9 aerial
127 Type 974 radar
128 Wind speed transmitter (starboard); wind direction transmitter (port)
129 Aerial outfits AYE, AYD and AYC
130 Type 984 radar
131 MK X IFF (identification friend or foe)
132 Turning light
133 Traffic lights

E3/2

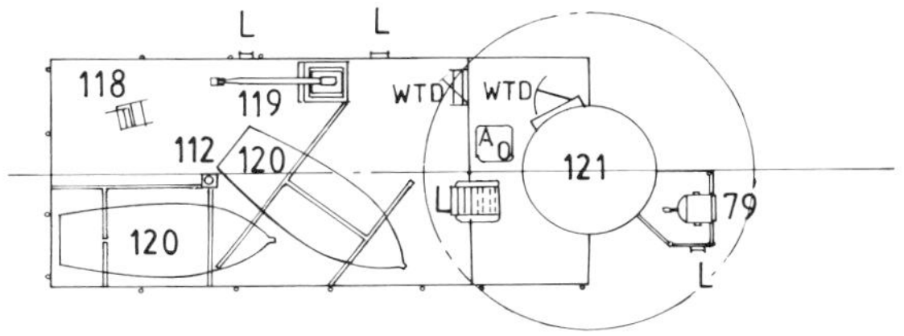

E3/3

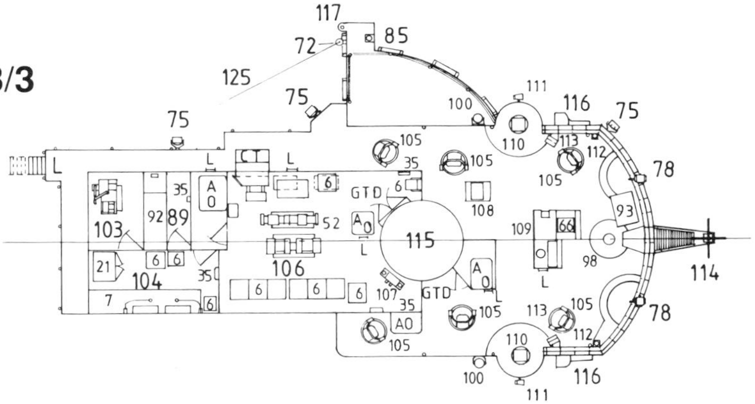

E3/4

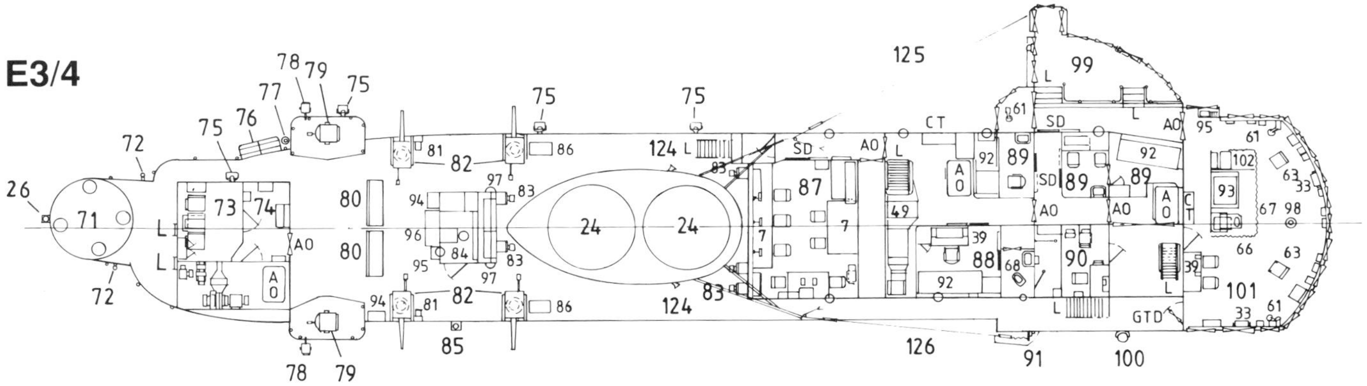

E3/2 Plan above C deck

E3/3 C deck

E3/4 B deck

E Superstructure

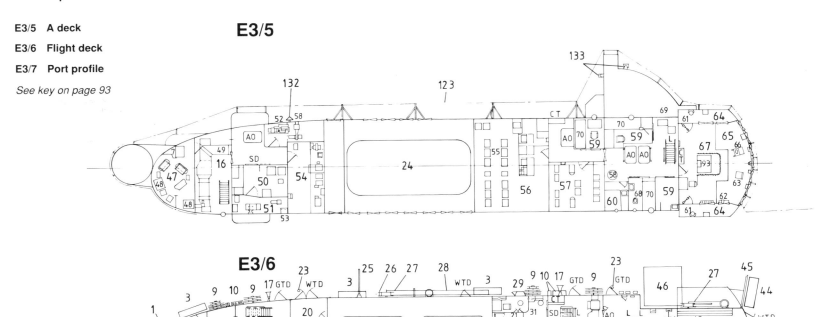

E3/5

E3/6

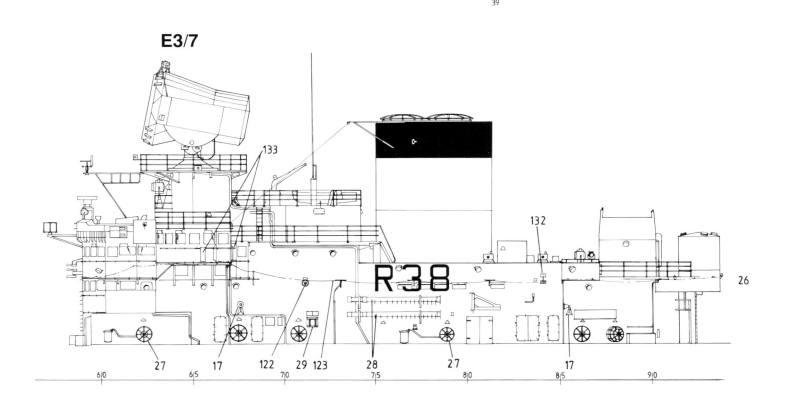

E3/7

R38

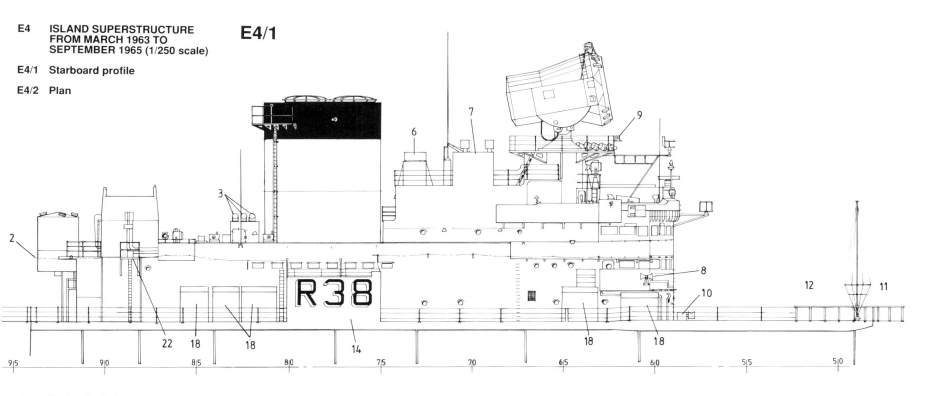

E4   ISLAND SUPERSTRUCTURE FROM MARCH 1963 TO SEPTEMBER 1965 (1/250 scale)

E4/1   Starboard profile

E4/2   Plan

E4/1

1	Obstruction light	
2	Magnetic loop broadcast	
3	Quartz iodine floodlights	
4	Crash landing floodlights (white)	
5	Traffic lights	
6	Cooling machinery	
7	Duplicate power supplies compartment for type 984 radar	
8	Loudspeakers	
9	Steaming light	
10	1½-ton electric winch	
11	AGG aerial	
12	Plastic guard rails and stanchions	
13	Mobile equipment and weapons platform	
14	Mobile equipment servicing station	
15	Drop tank stowage	
16	Loading rail	
17	Windscreen wiper	
18	Locker	
19	Whip aerial	
20	Emergency whip aerial	
21	Distant reading thermograph	
22	Aerial platform	

E4/2

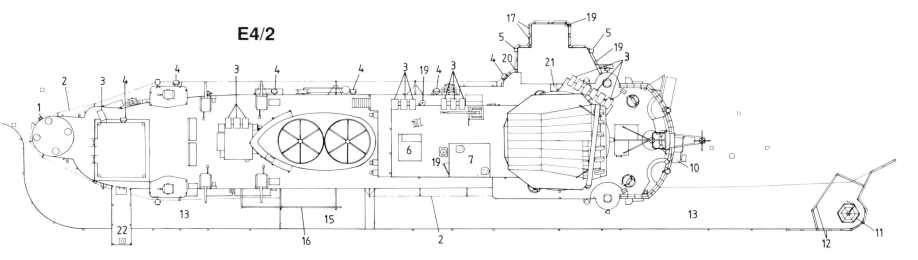

E Superstructure

E4/3   Port profile

See key on page 95

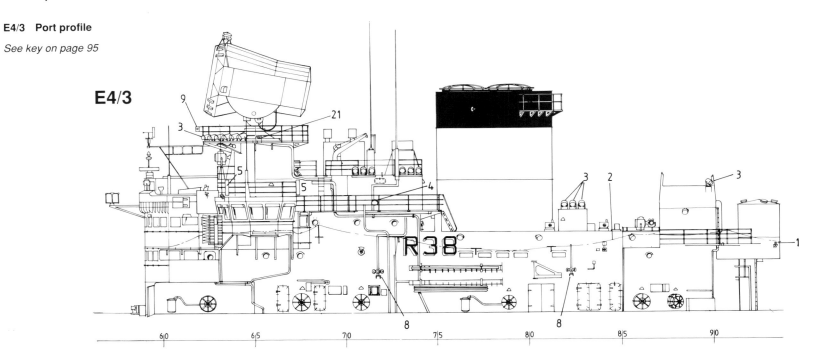

E4/3

**F1   FORWARD TRIPOD MAST AS
         FITTED (1/150 scale)**

F1/1   Starboard profile

F1/2   Front view

1	Type 79 air warning radar
2	Anemometer and wind vane
3	Thermograph
4	Gaff
5	Masthead flashing lamps
6	Direction finding H/F D/F coil
7	Visual flashing lantern position
8	Type 72 DM aircraft homing beacon
9	W/T yardarm (wireless telegraph)
10	Steaming light
11	Lantern
12	Signal yard
13	Yardarm flashing lantern

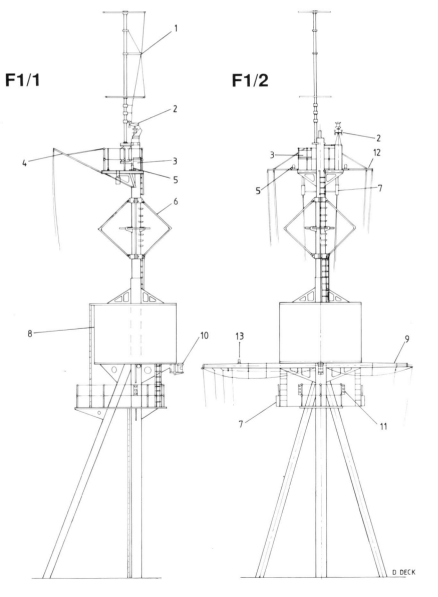

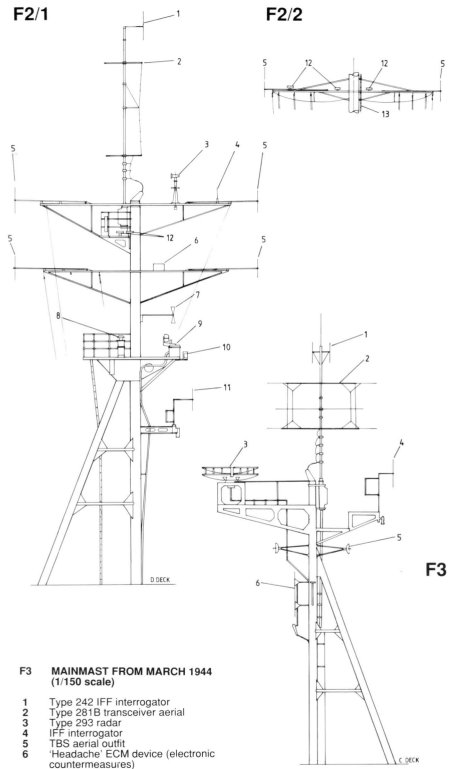

F2 **FORWARD TRIPOD MAST FROM MARCH 1944 (1/150 scale)**

F2/1 Starboard profile

F2/2 Front view of upper W/T yardarm

1 Type 272M IFF interrogator
2 Type 79B radar
3 Anemometer and wind vane
4 Type 251 surface radar beacon
5 TBS aerial outfit
6 Thermograph
7 Type 265 IFF responder
8 Daylight signalling lantern
9 American SG radar aerial
10 Steaming light
11 Type 242M responder
12 Flashing lights
13 Ladder

F2/1

F2/2

F1/1

F1/2

D DECK

D DECK

D DECK

F3

C DECK

F3 **MAINMAST FROM MARCH 1944 (1/150 scale)**

1 Type 242 IFF interrogator
2 Type 281B transceiver aerial
3 Type 293 radar
4 IFF interrogator
5 TBS aerial outfit
6 'Headache' ECM device (electronic countermeasures)

97

F Rig

F4 **MAINMAST AFTER
MODERNISATION** 1958
(1/150 scale)

F4/1 **Starboard profile**

F4/2 **Plan**

F4/1

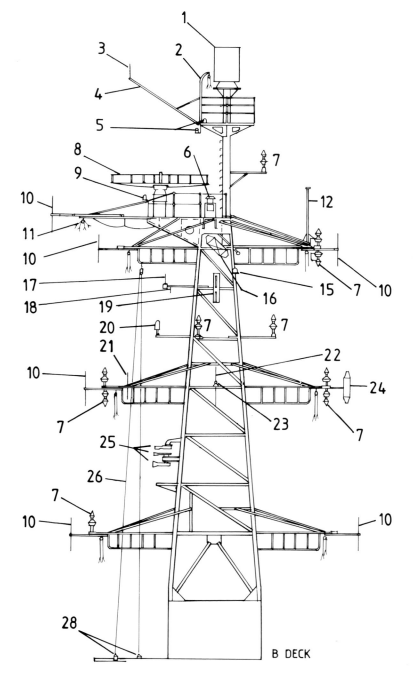

B DECK

F4/2

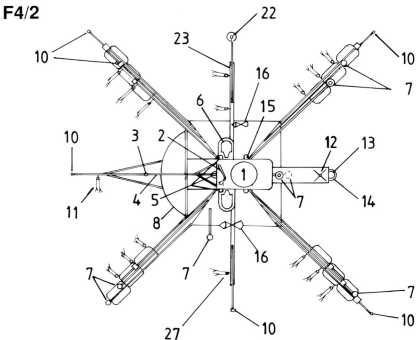

1	URN 3 aerial outfit AMG for type 957
2	Portable davit
3	Test aerial AMG URN3
4	Wood spur
5	Mast obstruction light
6	Daylight signalling lantern
7	Aerial outfit AJE
8	Type 293Q aerial outfit ANS
9	Admiral's toplight
10	Aerial outfit APH
11	Block for sea ensign
12	Polemast 8ft for Admiral's flag
13	Steaming light
14	Battery fed emergency steaming light
15	Flashing lantern
16	Aerial outfits AGA starboard, ANE port
17	AT 244/UPN-7
18	AEW test aerial
19	Antenna assembly AS 466/SR
20	Antenna AS 177/UPX/AMA for type 954
21	Merchant ship V/HF aerial (mid line)
22	Aerial outfit AJD port, APH starboard
23	Signal yard 30ft
24	Aerial outfit AJD
25	Aerial outfit AYE, AYD, AYC (mid line)
26	Receiving aerial to BWO
27	Block for flag halyards and not under control lights
28	Deck insulators

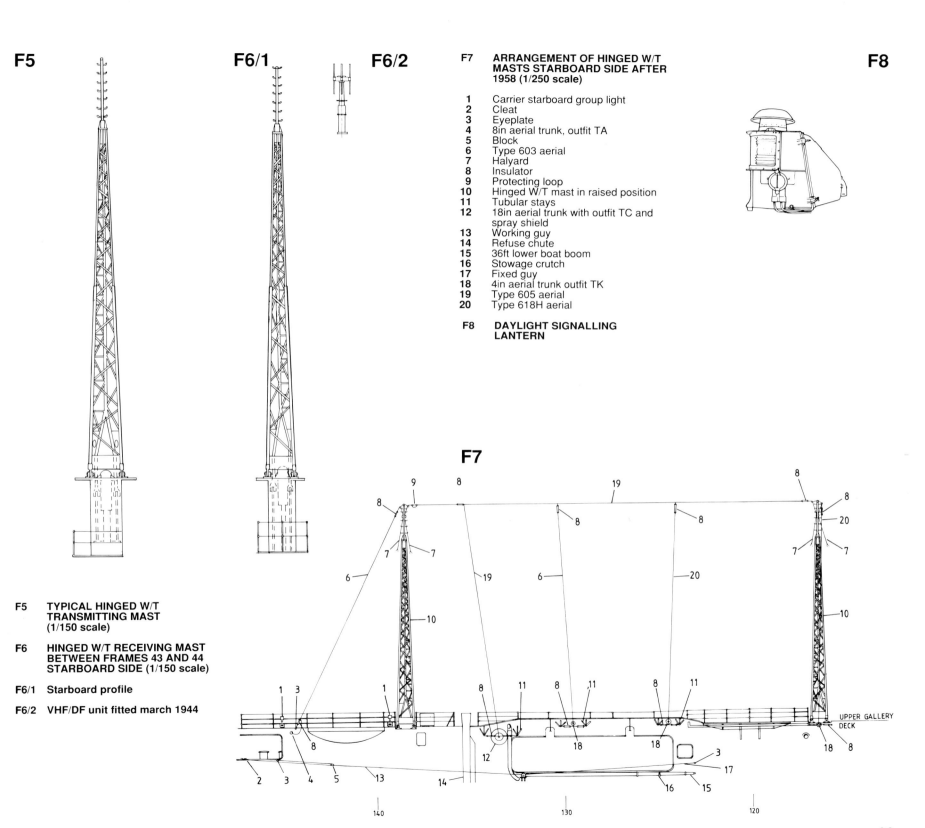

F5

F6/1   **F6/2**

F7 ARRANGEMENT OF HINGED W/T
MASTS STARBOARD SIDE AFTER
1958 (1/250 scale)

1   Carrier starboard group light
2   Cleat
3   Eyeplate
4   8in aerial trunk, outfit TA
5   Block
6   Type 603 aerial
7   Halyard
8   Insulator
9   Protecting loop
10   Hinged W/T mast in raised position
11   Tubular stays
12   18in aerial trunk with outfit TC and
spray shield
13   Working guy
14   Refuse chute
15   36ft lower boat boom
16   Stowage crutch
17   Fixed guy
18   4in aerial trunk outfit TK
19   Type 605 aerial
20   Type 618H aerial

F8   DAYLIGHT SIGNALLING
LANTERN

F8

F5   TYPICAL HINGED W/T
TRANSMITTING MAST
(1/150 scale)

F6   HINGED W/T RECEIVING MAST
BETWEEN FRAMES 43 AND 44
STARBOARD SIDE (1/150 scale)

F6/1   Starboard profile

F6/2   VHF/DF unit fitted march 1944

F7

UPPER GALLERY
DECK

140   130   120

F Rig

F9 WHIP AERIAL OPERATING GEAR

1 Whip aerial
2 Trunnion barrel
3 Cylinder
4 Vent valve
5 To/from main control valve
6 Cut off valve
7 Locking pin in stowed position
8 Combined ram and rack
9 From/to charging valve chest
10 Soleplate

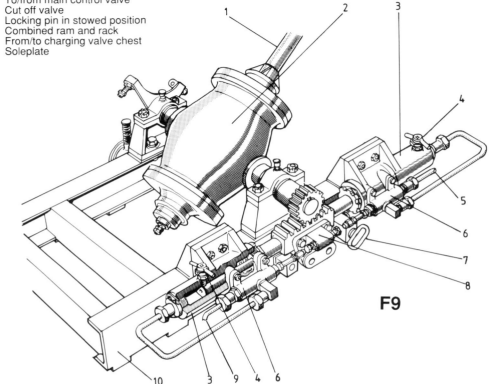

F9

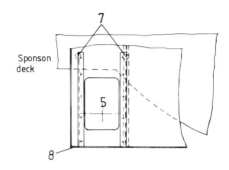

F10/5

F10/4

Sponson deck

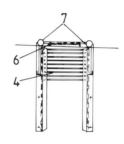

F10/3

F10 AERIAL OUTFIT AWL(M) AND BASE TUNER AT FRAME 144 STARBOARD, FITTED SEPTEMBER 1965 (1/50 scale)

F10/1 Elevation looking aft

F10/2 Elevation looking to port

F10/3 Plan of base tuner seating

F10/4 Plan of aerial seating

F10/5 Base tuner mounting brackets (1/33 scale)

1 Glass fibre spray shield
2 Base tuner outfit
3 Guard rails
4 Walkway
5 Centreline of whip aerial AWL(M)
6 Ladder
7 Pillar
8 Liquid oxygen stowage platform

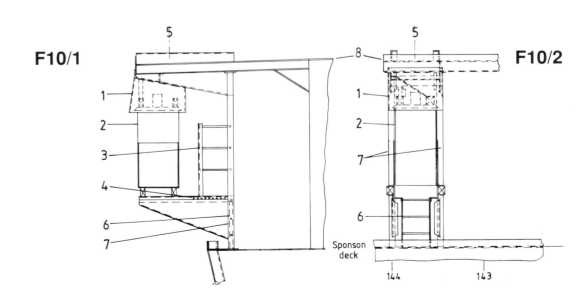

F10/1

F10/2

Sponson deck

144   143

F11 AERIAL OUTFIT AWL(M) AND BASE TUNER AT FRAME 150½ STARBOARD, FITTED SEPTEMBER 1965 (scale and key as for F10)

F11/1 Elevation looking aft

F11/2 Elevation looking to port

F11/3 Plan of aerial seating

F11/4 Plan of walkway

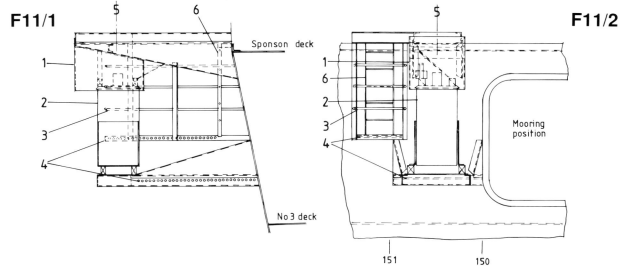

F11/1

Sponson deck

No 3 deck

F11/2

Mooring position

151   150

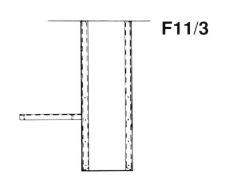

F11/3

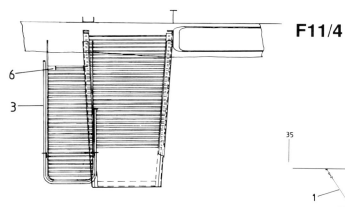

F11/4

F12/1

35   30   25

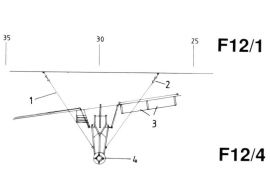

F12/4

F12 VHF/DF MAST FITTED 1958 IN OPERATING POSITION STARBOARD SIDE (1/250 scale)

F12/1 Plan

F12/2 Starboard profile

F12/3 Front view

F12/4 UHF/DF aerial plan and profile (fitted August 1960)

1   Stay
2   Screwslip
3   20-man life raft and survival pack
4   Aerial antenna unit DES
5   Access platform

F12/2

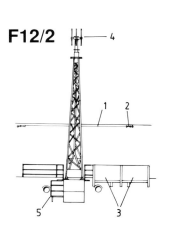

F12/3

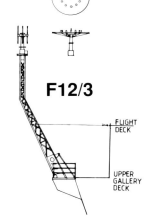

FLIGHT DECK

UPPER GALLERY DECK

G Armament

G1 4.5IN HA/LA BETWEEN DECK
TWIN MOUNTING MK II
(1/50 scale)

G1/1 Plan of starboard side upper
gallery deck and flight deck after
mountings

G1/2 Plan between upper gallery deck
and flight deck

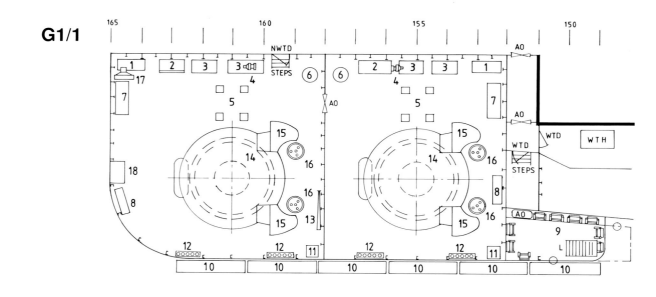

G1/1

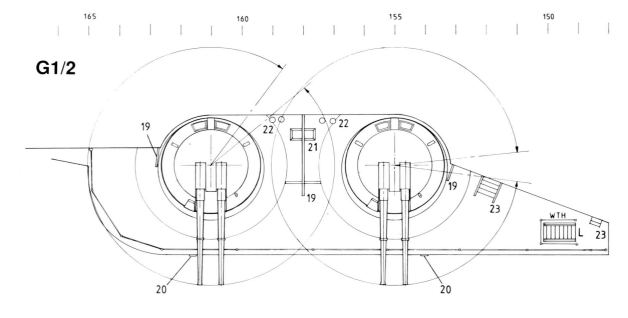

G1/2

1	Oil tank	**12**	Drill cartridges
2	Star shell ready-use locker	**13**	2pdr sub calibre for 4.5in HA guns
3	High explosive shell ready-use locker	**14**	4.5in MK II mounting
4	Exhaust fan	**15**	Loading access steps
5	Drill loading tray and pads	**16**	Revolving three-round scuttle
6	Ammunition hoist	**17**	Supply fan
7	Semi armour piercing ready-use locker	**18**	Steel bench
8	Periscope stowed position	**19**	Ramp
9	Bomb trolleys	**20**	Foot rung
10	Flotanets	**21**	Pyrene generators
11	Clearance charges	**22**	Pyrene cylinders
		23	Mild steel ladder

G1/3   Profile starboard side

G1/4   Section looking aft

G1/3

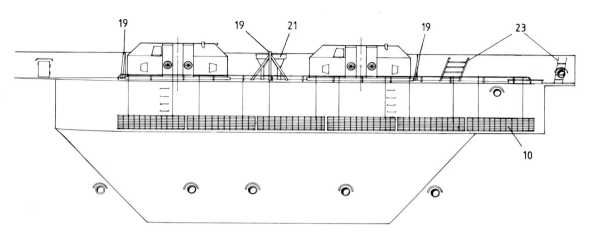

G1/4

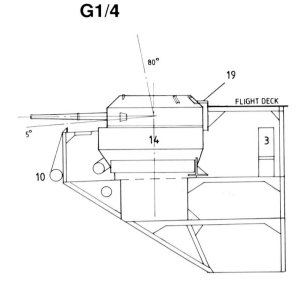

G2   GENERAL VIEW OF 4.5in HA/LA MK II BD MOUNTING WITH SHIELD REMOVED

G2

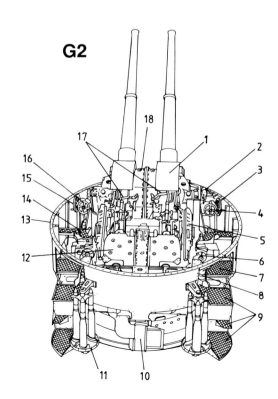

1	Mantlet plate
2	Training receiver
3	Trainer's manual handwheel
4	Trainer's power drive handwheel
5	Loading tray
6	Fuse setting machine
7	Gun house deck level
8	Fuse setting tray
9	Loading access steps
10	Ventilation fan and trunking
11	Revolving three round scuttle
12	Balance weight
13	Securing flange for upper portion of gunhouse
14	Breech-worker's platform
15	Layer's manual handwheel
16	Layer's power drive handwheel
17	Quick fire and semi automatic lever
18	Gun cradle

G Armament

G3 **GENERAL ARRANGEMENT OF 4.5in HA/LA BD MOUNTING MK II** (1/75 scale)

G3/1 **Left elevation**

G3/2 **Right elevation**

G3/3 **Plan**

1 Loading tray
2 Lever operating ammunition stand
3 Air bottle
4 Balance weight
5 Recuperator
6 Elevation receiver
7 Hand elevator
8 Hand trainer
9 Training receiver

G3/1

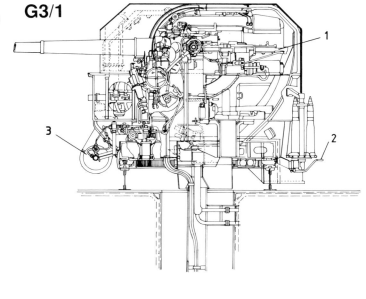

G3/2

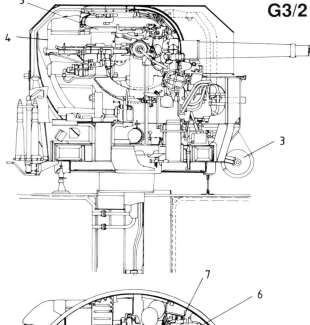

G4 **MULTIPLE MK VIA 2pdr POM-POM MOUNTING**

G3/3

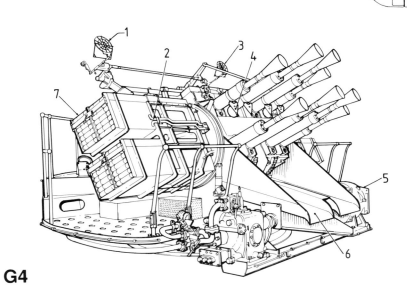

G4

1 Trainer's sight
2 Interrupter handles
3 Layer's sight
4 Cartridge diverter
5 Electric motor
6 Empty cartridge chute
7 Ammunition magazine

G5 3pdr SALUTING GUN (1/50 scale)

G6 20mm SINGLE OERLIKON MOUNTING (1/50 scale)

G7 40mm BOFORS QUADRUPLE MOUNTING MK 2 (1/50 scale)

G7/1 Left elevation

G7/2 Front view

G7/3 Plan

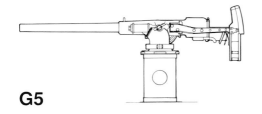

G5

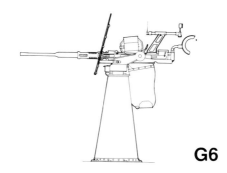

G6

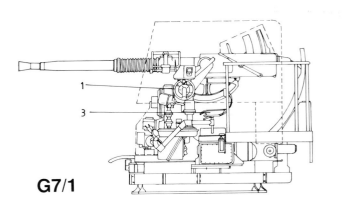

G7/1

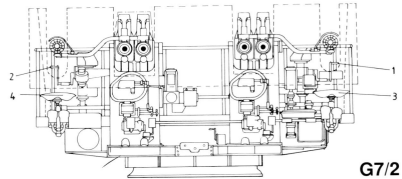

G7/2

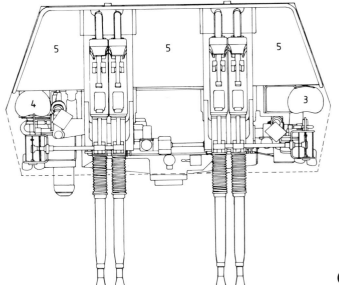

G7/3

1	Elevating crank
2	Training crank
3	Pointer's seat
4	Trainer's seat
5	Loading platform

G Armament

G8 **40mm BOFORS TWIN MOUNT MK 1** (1/50 scale – key as for G7)

G8/1 Plan

G8/2 Left elevation

G8/3 Right elevation

G8/4 Front view

G8/1

G8/3

G8/2

G8/4

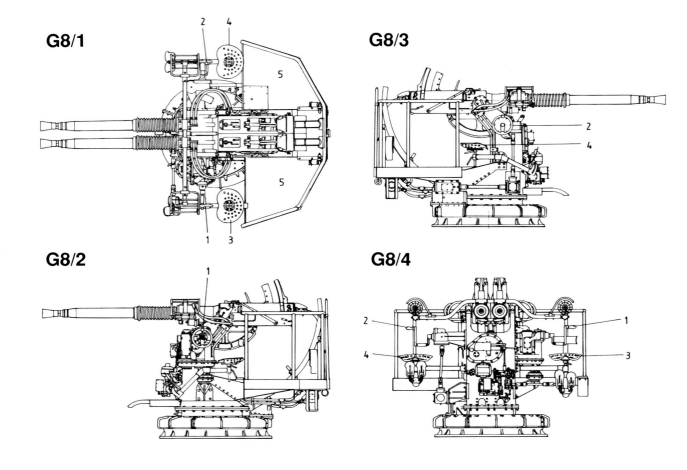

G9 **40mm BOFORS SINGLE MOUNT MK 3**

G9/1 Plan

G9/2 Left elevation

G9/3 Rear view

G9/4 Front view

G9/1

G9/3

G9/2

G9/4

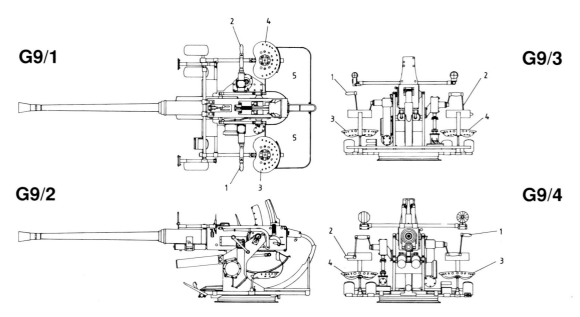

**G10   AFTER GUN PLATFORM ADDED
JANUARY 1943 (1/250 scale)**

G10/1 Stern view

G10/2 Starboard profile

G10/3 Plan

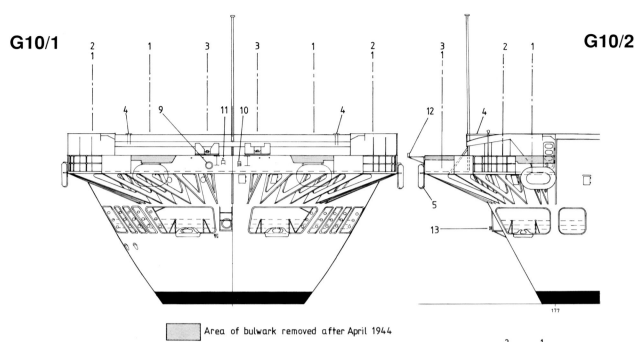

G10/1

G10/2

Area of bulwark removed after April 1944

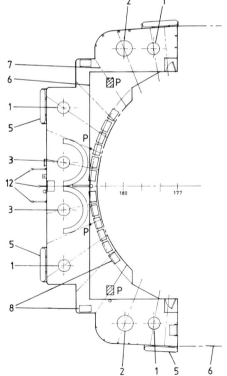

G10/3

1	20mm single Oerlikon, replaced by 20mm twin Oerlikon April 1944
2	44in searchlight, replaced by 40mm Bofors mounting MK 3 June 1945
3	20mm single Oerlikon, fitted January 1943
4	Outrigger for aircraft tailwheel
5	Carley float
6	Line of flight deck over
7	Line of brackets under
8	Ready-use ammunition lockers
9	Fog light
10	Stern light
11	Overtaking light
12	Admiral's light
13	Lower stern light

G Armament

G11/1

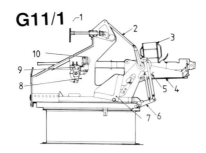

G11/2

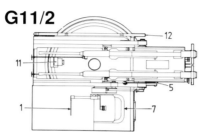

G11   20mm TWIN MK V OERLIKON MOUNTING (1/50 scale)

G11/1 Profile

G11/2 Plan

1	Cartwheel foresight
2	Sight link
3	Magazine
4	Firing rod
5	Firing can
6	Fire interruptor operating lever
7	Layer's seat
8	Firing valve
9	Elevating valve
10	Control handle
11	Training motor
12	Cocking lever

G13   3in/50cal MK 33 TWIN MOUNTING (1/50 scale)

G13/1 Plan

G13/2 Left profile

G13/3 Plan cutaway

G13/4 Left front view of carriage

1	Local surface control seat
2	Right loading platform
3	Mount captain's seat
4	Centre loading platform
5	Left loading platform
6	Local AA fire control seat
7	Train centring pin
8	Control panel
9	Fixed ejection chute
10	Left gun carriage pedestal
11	Water inlet tube
12	Ready-use magazine
13	Electric motor
14	Train pinion
15	Bevel gear housing
16	Brake release mechanism
17	Manual drive switch
18	Outline of shield
19	Fire interrupter

G12

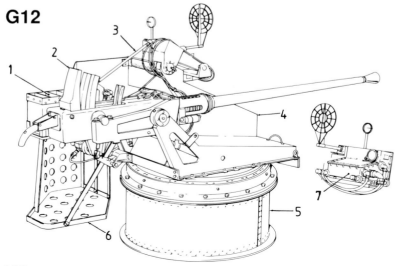

G12   40mm 'BOFFIN' GUN MK V

1	Ammunition stowage
2	Shot guides
3	Sight link
4	Layer's cab
5	Fixed structure
6	Loader's platform
7	Gyro sight MK XIV and open sight

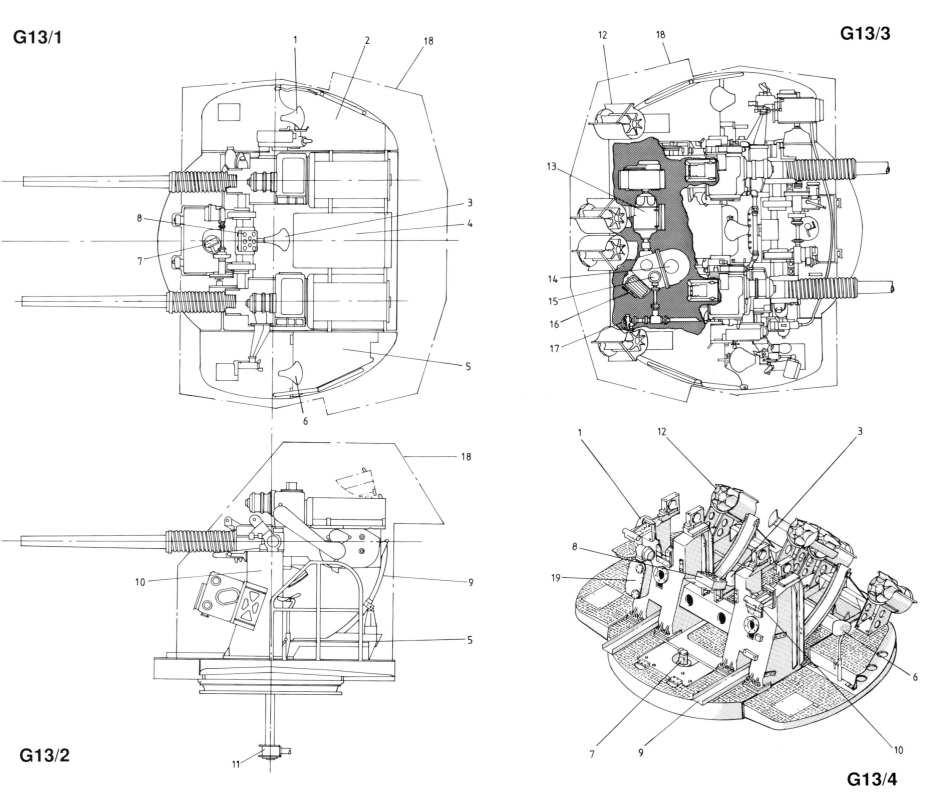

G13/1

G13/2

G13/3

G13/4

G Armament

G14/1

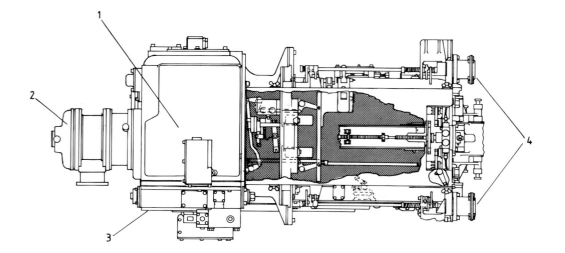

G14 **3IN LOADER MK2 MOD 3**
(1/15 scale)

G14/1 **Plan**

G14/2 **Left profile**

G14/3 **Rear view**

1   Loader drive housing
2   Electric motor
3   Drive chain cover
4   Solenoid plunger and linkage
5   Firing solenoid

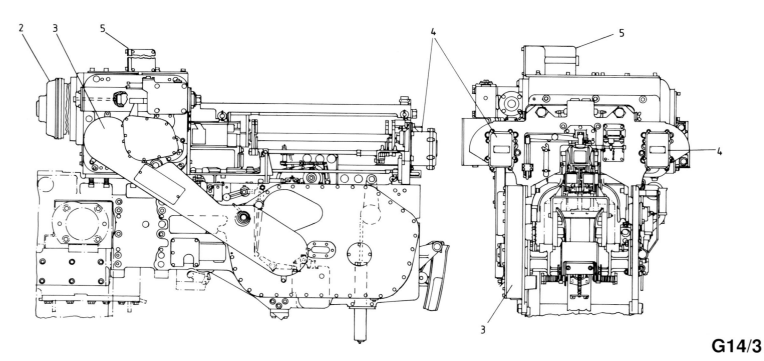

G14/2

G14/3

G15 MOUNT CAPTAIN'S CONTROLS

1 Left loader indicator panel
2 Selector ASF
3 Selector GSS
4 Selector FSS
5 Right loader indicator panel
6 Gun captain's key
7 Right loader master push button
8 Gun laying emergency stop control
9 Left loader master push button

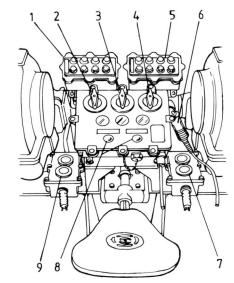

G15

G16 RADAR ANTENNA INSTALLATION ON 3in MOUNT

G16/1 Front view

G16/2 Side view

1 Paraboloidal reflector
2 Antenna wave guide feed
3 Antenna yoke
4 Wave guide
5 Antenna elevation cylinder
6 Antenna mount frame
7 Antenna traverse control box
8 Loader drive unit main housing
9 Loader drive electric motor
10 Antenna drive pump and sump unit
11 Antenna elevation control box
12 Scanning drive motor and reference generator

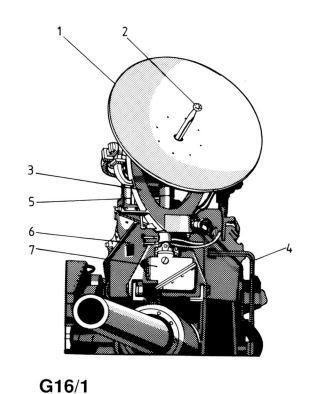

G16/1

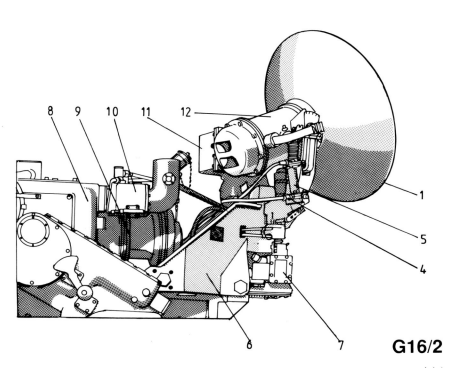

G16/2

G Armament

G17/1

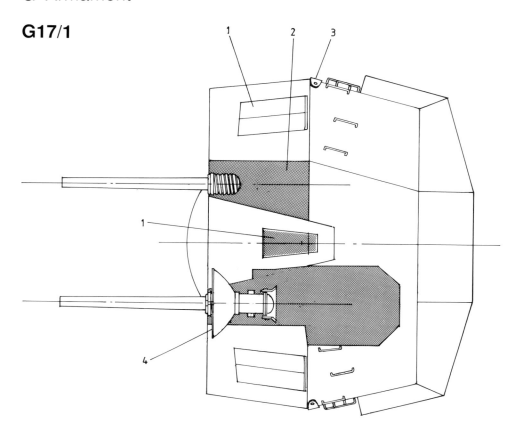

G17 **3in/50cal MK 33 SHIELD ARRANGEMENT (1/50 scale)**

G17/1 **Plan**

G17/2 **Left profile**

G17/3 **Front view**

1 Sight port
2 Canvas
3 Eyelift
4 Radar antenna
5 Climbing rungs
6 Door
7 Ejection chute

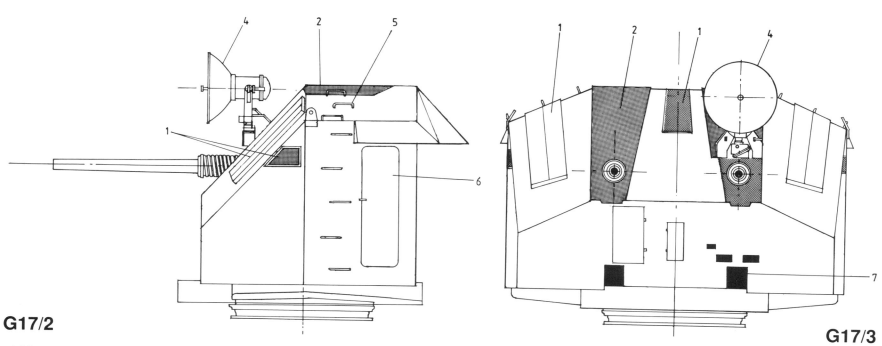

G17/2

G17/3

H Fittings

H1	QUARTERDECK AS FITTED (1/250 scale)			1	Stern boom
				2	Lower shaded stern light
H1/1	**Plan**			3	Lower fog light
				4	Platform
H1/2	**Starboard profile**			5	Stowed position for stern boom
				6	Stream anchor
H1/3	**Section at after capstan**			7	Transporting rail
				8	Towing fairlead
H1/4	**Plan of capstan machinery on upper deck**			9	Splash bombing target
				10	Smoke floats (stowed)
				11	Deck clench
				12	20in bollard
				13	Life floats
				14	¾-ton winch for splash target
				15	Kisbie lifebuoy
				16	Night lifebuoy
				17	Washdeck locker
				18	Controller for winch
				19	Portable plate
				20	Capstan
				21	Ship's bell
				22	Signal to submarines ready-use locker
				23	Hawser reel

H2	HANGAR DECK AS FITTED BETWEEN FRAMES 139 and 151, 119 and 121, 88 and 97 and 37 and 61 (1/250 scale)	1	Mooring fairlead
		2	Hinged platform
H2/1	**Plan port side, 139 to 151**	3	Dope and acetone ready-use locker
		4	Hangar inductor
H2/2	**Plan starboard side, 139 to 151**	5	Accommodation locker
		6	18in bollard
H2/3	**Starboard profile, 139 to 151**	7	Wash deck locker
		8	Hawser reel
		9	1½-ton winch
		10	Nameplate
		11	Supply fan

H2/1

H2/2

H2/3

H1/1

H1/2

H1/3

H1/4

12	Refuse chute
13	Watertight armoured hatch
14	Exhaust fan
15	Seaplane boom
16	Cleat
17	Portable petrol pump
18	Armour door
19	Flotanet
20	Bollard
21	Drifter ladder (stowed)
22	3-ton winch
23	MK VII paravane
24	Gallows crane rotating gear
25	Paravane transporting rail
26	Gallows crane
27	Lower boom (stowed)
28	Plane unit
29	Ladder (stowed over)
30	Drifter ladder rigged
31	Dumping platform

WTD	Watertight door
V	Vent
WTH	Watertight hatch
AO	Access opening
L	Ladder

H Fittings

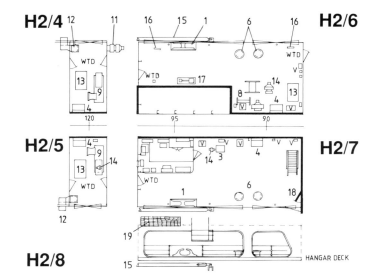

H2/4   **H2/6**

H2/5   **H2/7**

H2/8

HANGAR DECK

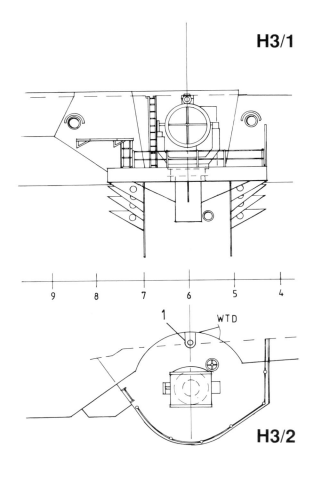

H3/1

H3/2

H2/9

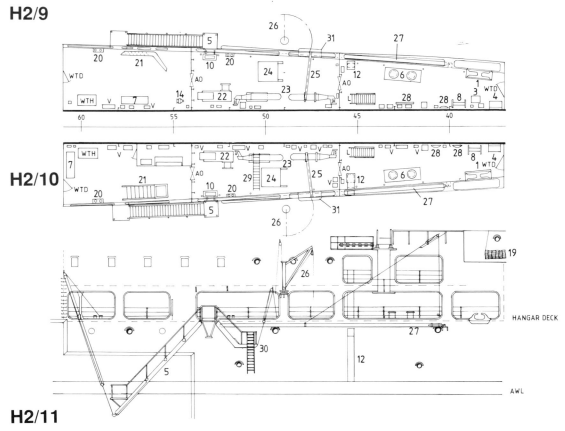

H2/10

HANGAR DECK

AWL

H2/11

114

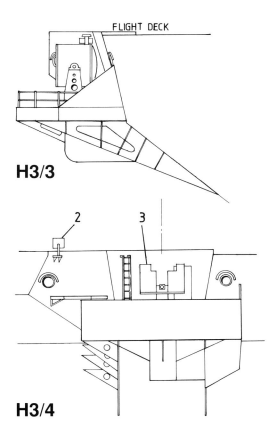

FLIGHT DECK

H3/3

H3/4

H4 **20in SIGNALLING PROJECTOR LIGHT**

1 Eyepiece
2 Signalling handle
3 Ventilating motor
4 Telescope with eyepiece

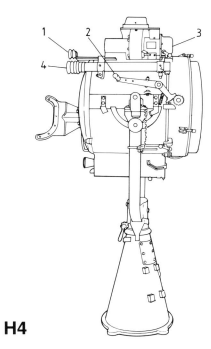

H4

H5 **10in SIGNALLING PROJECTOR LIGHT (1/10 scale)**

H5/1 **Right profile**

H5/2 **Sectioned front view**

H5/3 **Left profile**

1 Eye piece
2 Signalling handle
3 Shutters
4 Lamp
5 Power cable

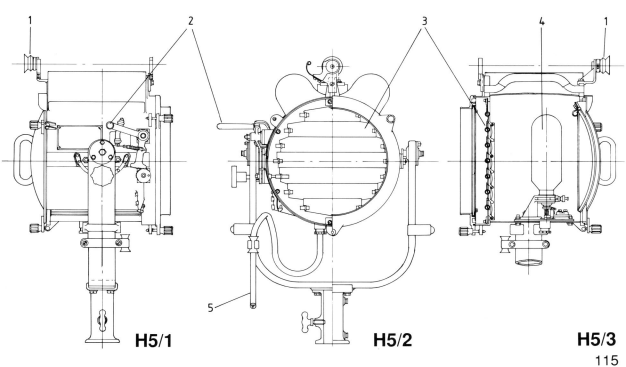

H5/1   **H5/2**   **H5/3**

H Fittings

H6 CAMOUFLAGE PATTERN, PORT SIDE FROM 1941 TO 1943

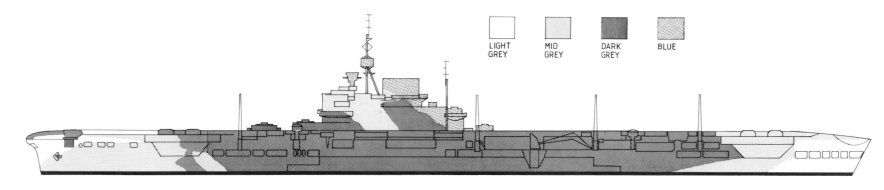

LIGHT GREY MID GREY DARK GREY BLUE

H6

H7 QUARTERDECK AFTER MODERNISATION 1958 (1/250 scale)

H7/1 Starboard profile

H7/2 Plan

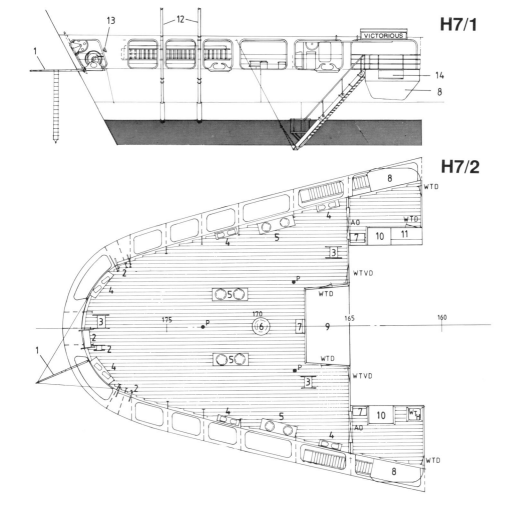

H7/1

H7/2

1 Stern boom
2 Reel
3 Hawser reel
4 Fairlead
5 Bollards
6 Capstan
7 Desk
8 Accommodation ladder and brow platform
9 Quarter deck locker
10 Jigger trunk
11 Quarter deck part of ship locker
12 Scuppers
13 Stern anchor light
14 Hanging jumping ladder stowage

AO Access opening
P Pillar
WTD Watertight door
WTVD Watertight ventilation door

H8 **EXTERNAL FITTINGS ON UPPER GALLERY DECK AND FLIGHT DECK AFTER MODERNISATION** (1/250 scale)

H8/1 Starboard profile after frame 160

H8/2 Flight deck plan after frame 160

H8/3 Flight deck plan between frames 152 and 162

H8/4 Starboard profile between frames 152 and 162

1	Admiral's stern light
2	Safety net
3	Fog light, shaded stern light and emergency overtaking light
4	Grated walkway
5	14ft dinghy
6	Whip aerial
7	Portable ensign staff
8	Double stowed survival pack and liferaft
9	Methanol tank
10	Stanchion
11	Loudspeaker flight deck broadcast (removed after March 1963)
12	Aircraft fuelling position (AVCAT)
13	Ready-use locker for engine starter cartridges
14	Foam locker
15	Reels for engine starter cables
16	Aircraft electrical servicing position
17	Hinged servicing bench
18	Outline light (white)
19	Gutterway
20	Round-down lights (white)
21	Single survival pack and liferaft
22	Scuppers
23	Magnetic loop broadcast
24	Deck landing mirror sight source lights
25	Deck surface light
26	Arrester wire
27	Group OC insulator
28	3in/50cal twin mounting
29	Carrier group light
30	Mk 63 director
31	Ammunition davit
32	Simplex floodlight
33	Wash deck locker
34	Reels for aircraft servicing cables
35	Ready-use ammunition lockers
36	Ammunition hoist
37	1½-ton electric winch
38	8in aerial trunk
39	Hinged W/T mast in lowered (operating) position
40	Locker
41	Refuse chute
42	Reel
43	Emergency crash barrier mast in lowered (stowed) position
44	Weapon lift cover
45	Weapon lift switch gear
46	Ready-use nylon pack
47	Handwheel operating valves in Avcat filter unit under
48	Portable tripod for light stores (until November 1963)

Key continued on page 118

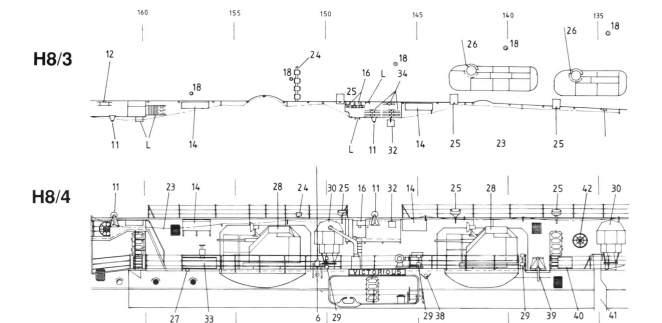

H Fittings

Continued from page 117

49 Portable stump mast for heavy stores
50 Deck landing mirror sight
51 Contour light axial deck (red)
52 35ft medium speed boat
53 Boat crutches
54 18in aerial trunk
55 Boat davits
56 CRBF director
57 4in aerial trunk
58 Diesel generator exhaust pipe
59 Weapon lift hatch
60 40mm six-barrelled Bofors
61 Hinged W/T mast
62 Emergency whip aerial
63 VHF/DF DES2 antenna unit
64 Bridle stowages
65 Avcat filters
66 Directing officer's lamp box
67 Carrier identification lights
68 Pilotage bow light
69 Forward portable stump mast after November 1963
70 Hose racks
71 Aircraft electrical servicing positions after November 1963
72 Liferaft stowages removed after November 1963
73 Fore and aft indicator mast in rigged position
74 Fore and aft indicator mast in stowed position
75 Ammonia locker removed after November 1963
76 Drum for catapult track sealing strip
77 Anemometer transmitter added after November 1963
78 Anchor light
79 Bridle catcher and control position for parking chocks
80 Axial deck end light (amber)
81 Portable jackstaff
82 Forward portable tripod mast for light stores after November 1963
83 Axial deck centreline lights (white)
84 Ammonia lockers
85 Foam locker removed after November 1963
86 Ready-use lockers added after November 1963
87 Whip aerial added after November 1963
88 Platform for aircraft starter operator
89 Ammunition hoist platform removed after November 1963
90 Angled deck end light (amber)
91 Angled flight deck centreline light (white)

Key continued on page 119

H8/5

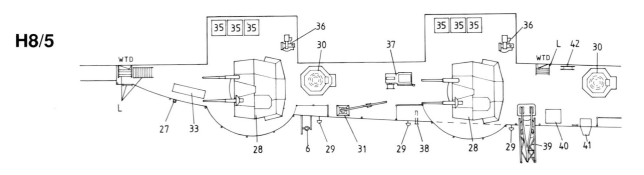

H8/6

H8/7

H8/8

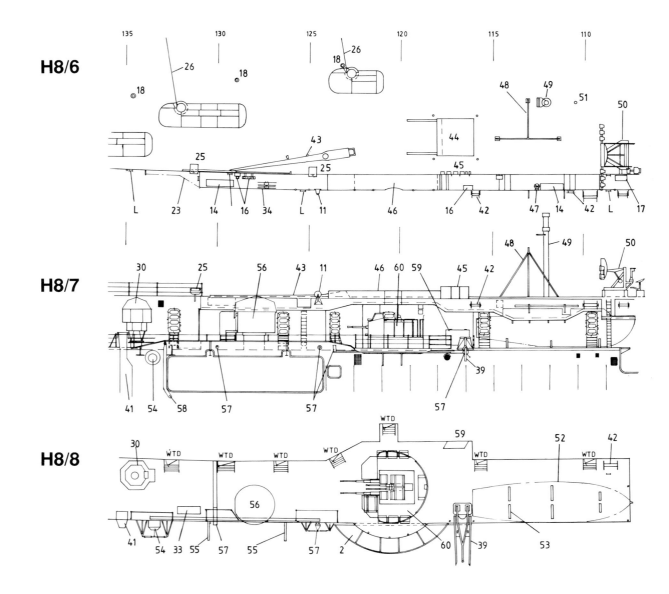

H8/9 Flight deck plan between frames 22 and 58

H8/10 Starboard profile between frames 22 and 58

H8/11 Upper gallery deck plan between frames 22 and 58

Continued from page 118

92 Contour light angled flight deck (red)
93 Aircraft wheel chocks
94 Turning lights
95 Foam locker added after November 1963
96 Whip aerials added after November 1963
97 Stowage for oil transfer hoses
98 Hawser reels (over)
99 Hydraulic control valves for whip aerials
100 Arrester gear and emergency barrier control room
101 Single liferafts changed to doubles after November 1963
102 Collapsible roller fairlead cover

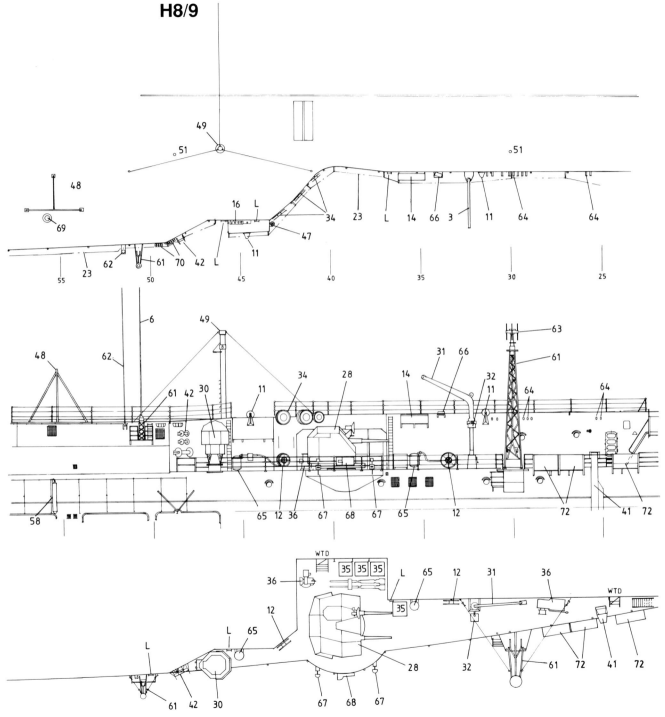

H Fittings

H8/12 Starboard profile forward of frame 25

H8/13 Flight deck plan forward of frame 25

See key pages 117–19

H8/12

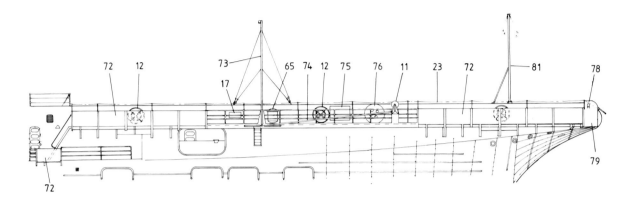

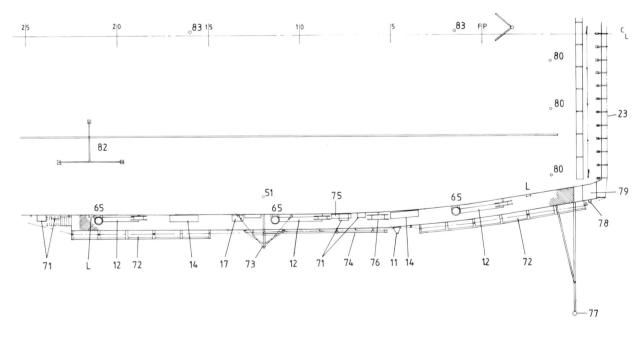

H8/13

H8/14 Flight deck plan forward of frame 24

H8/15 Port profile forward of frame 24

See key pages 117–19

H8/14

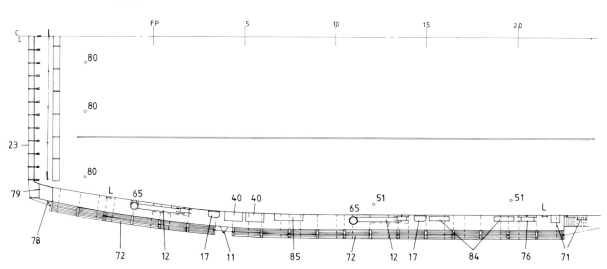

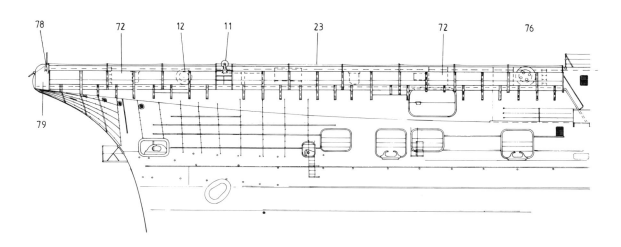

H8/15

H Fittings

H8/16 Flight deck plan between frames 19 and 55

H8/17 Port profile between frames 19 and 55

H8/18 Upper gallery deck plan between frames 19 and 55

See key pages 117–19

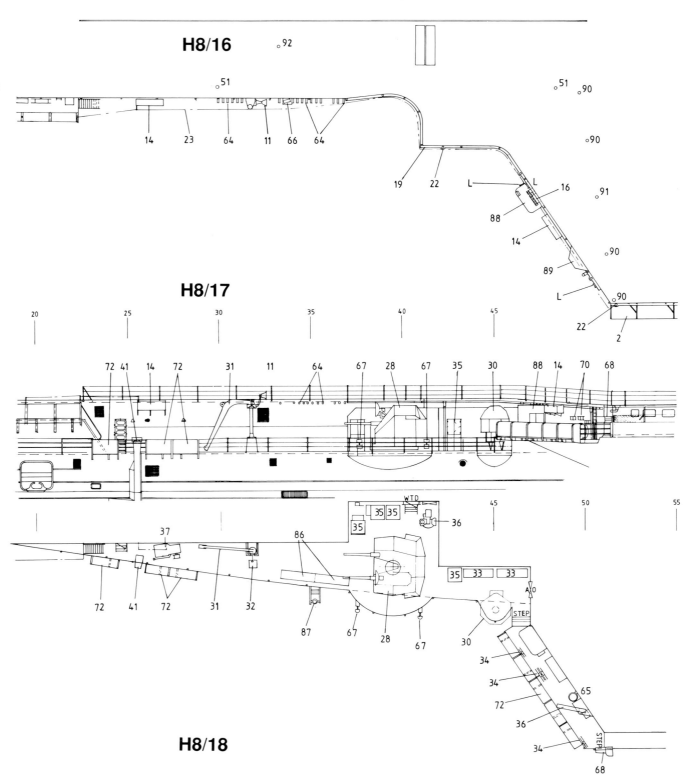

H8/16

H8/17

H8/18

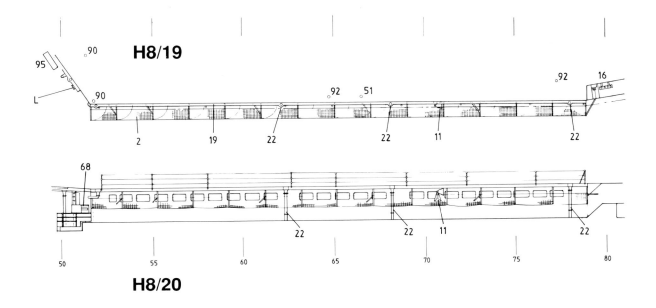

H8/19

H8/20

H8/21

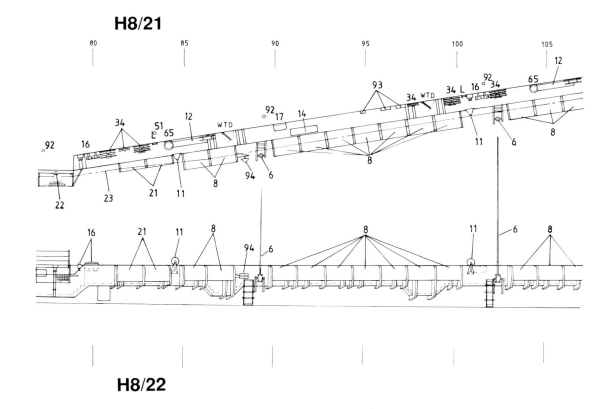

H8/22

H Fittings

H8/23 Upper gallery deck plan between frames 106 and 136

H8/24 Port profile between frames 106 and 136

H8/25 Flight deck plan between frames 106 and 136

See key pages 117–19

H8/23

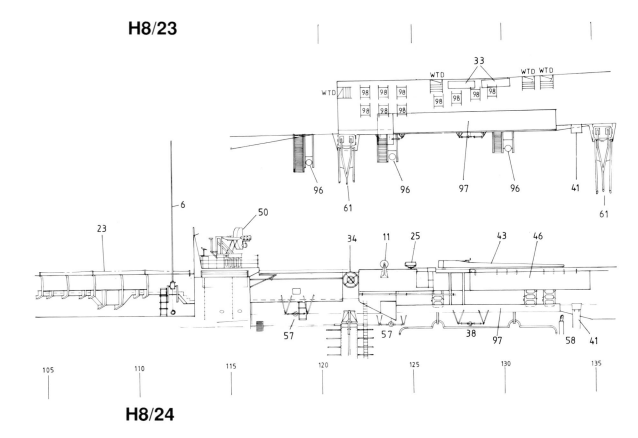

H8/24

H8/25

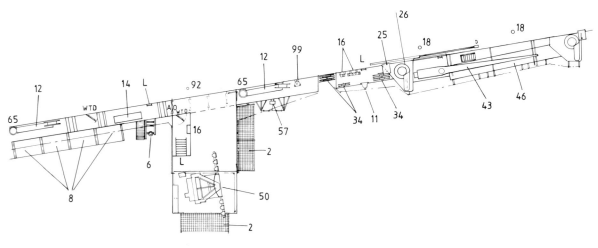

H8/26 Flight deck plan between frames 130 and 163

H8/27 Port profile between frames 130 and 163

H8/28 Upper gallery deck plan between frames 130 and 163

See key pages 117–19

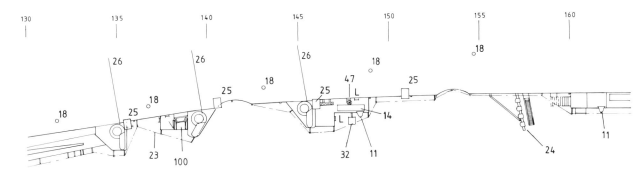

H8/26

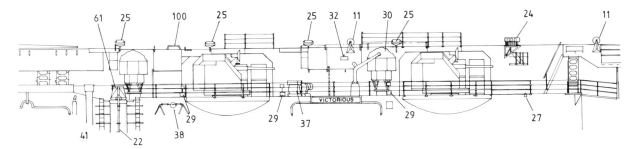

H8/27

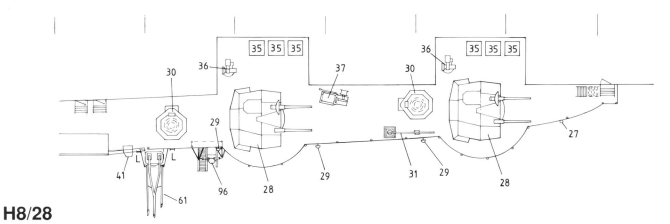

H8/28

125

H Fittings

H8/29 Flight deck plan aft of frame 158

H8/30 Port profile aft of frame 158

See key pages 117–19

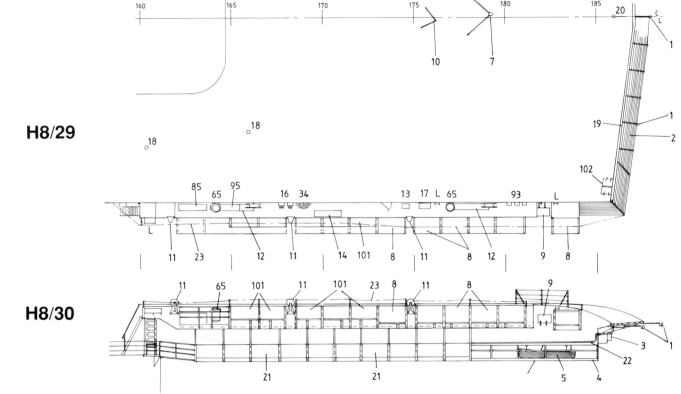

H8/29

H8/30

H9   **BALLOON FILLING STATION ADDED 1961 (1/250 scale)**

H9/1   **Plan of flight deck**

H9/2   **Port profile**

H9/3   **Stern view**

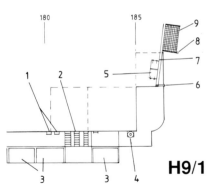

H9/1

1	Aircraft wheel chocks
2	Steps
3	Liferaft stowages
4	Gas bottle
5	Cover to collapsible roller fairlead
6	Scupper
7	Gutterway
8	Admiral's stern light
9	Safety net
10	Magnetic broadcast loop
11	Grated walkway
12	MT gas tank
13	Ring for holding inflated balloon

I1   **160cwt BYERS STOCKLESS ANCHOR (1/100 scale)**

I1/1   **Front elevation**

I1/2   **Side elevation**

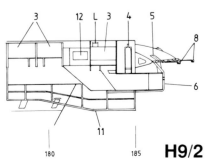

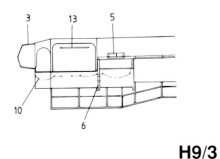

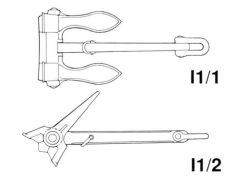

H9/2

H9/3

I1/1

I1/2

I3 PLAN OF CABLE DECK AS FITTED (1/250 scale) **I2**

1 Electrical ready-use and paravane gear store
2 Cordage reel (over)
3 Hawser reel
4 Mooring fairlead
5 Washdeck locker
6 Bollard
7 3pdr saluting gun
8 Locker for blank saluting ammunition
9 Cable holder
10 Deck pipe
11 Telescopic steaming light
12 Capstan
13 Chafing plate
14 Bell (over)
15 Scuttle
16 Clump cathead
17 Trolley
18 Bottle-screw slip
19 Blake slip
20 Eye plate
21 Wood rack (over)
22 Forecastle locker (over)
23 Towing fairlead
24 Typhon whistle
25 Bar shoes (stowed)
26 Paravane fairlead
27 Planning shoe stowage
28 Paint stage store (over)
29 Deck casting
30 Chain pipe
31 Clench plate
32 Inductor fan
33 Paraffin tank
34 Bosun's ready-use store
35 Blanks for deck pipes stowed

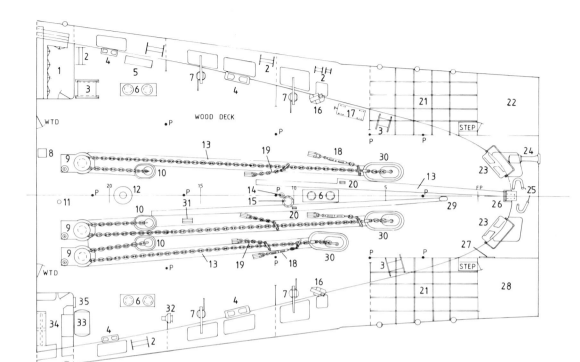

I3 FORWARD CAPSTAN GEAR WITH SHEET CABLE HOLDER (1/100 scale)

I3/1 Sectioned elevation

I3/2 Plan at upper deck

I3/3 Plan at lower gallery deck

1 Brake handwheel
2 Cable holder
3 Capstan
4 Electric motor
5 Centrifugal brake
6 Magnetic brake
7 Clutch gears
8 Spur wheels
9 Worm wheels
10 Sheet cable holder

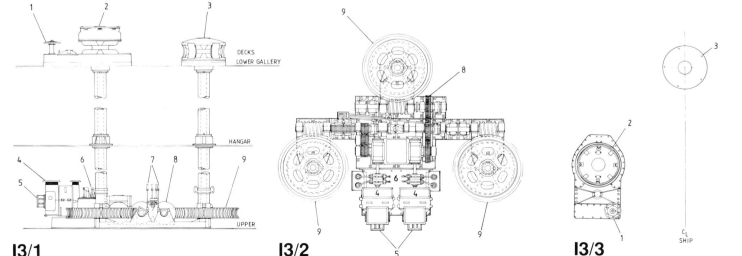

I3/1 I3/2 I3/3

J Boats

J1   **ARRANGEMENT OF BOATS ON LOWER GALLERY DECK AS FITTED (1/250 Scale)**

J1/1   **Port side between frames 121 and 151**

J1/2   **Starboard side between frames 121 and 151**

J1/3   **Section at frame 132**

J1/4   **Section at frame 119**

J1/1

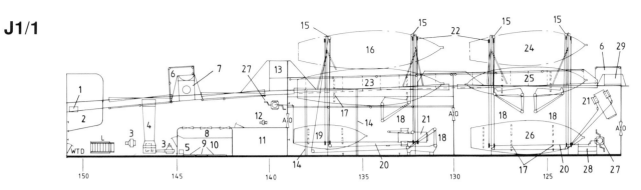

J1/2

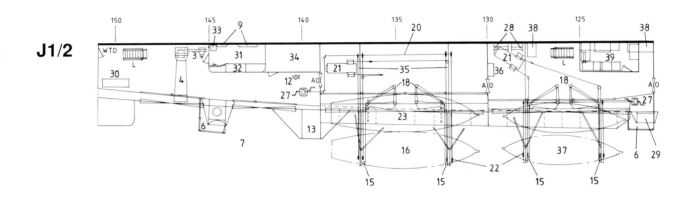

J1/3   **J1/4**

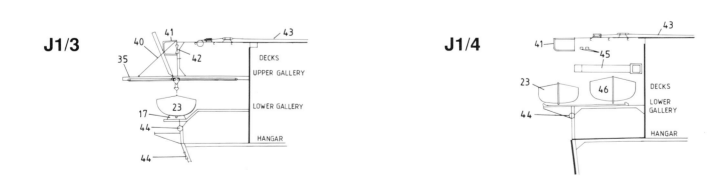

J1/5   Port side between frames 97 and 121

J1/6   Starboard side between frames 97 and 121

J1/5

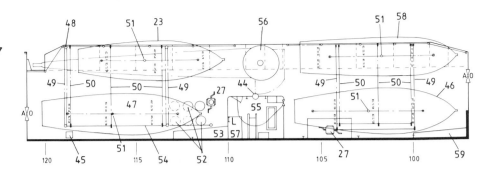

J1/6

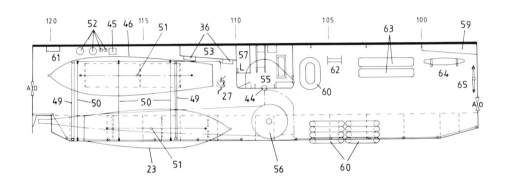

1	Hatch (over)	**33**	Tank for cleaning gear
2	Coal bunker	**34**	No 8 RDF office
3	Exhaust fan	**35**	Boat beam
4	Inductor (over)	**36**	Lifejacket locker
5	Waste bin	**37**	27ft whaler (lowering position)
6	Grating	**38**	Food lift
7	No 3 transmitting mast	**39**	Diving gear store
8	Workbench	**40**	Portable stay
9	Rods	**41**	Safety net
10	Shipwright's ready-use boat store	**42**	Rectangular port
11	No 9 RDF office	**43**	Arrester wire
12	Supply fan	**44**	Sidelight
13	Searchlight platform (over)	**45**	Aerial trunks
14	Rail (over)	**46**	36ft motor pinnace
15	Sheave	**47**	35ft fast motor boat
16	32ft life cutter (lowering position)	**48**	Chain guide wheels
17	Boat chocks	**49**	Chain
18	Shock absorber	**50**	Rail
19	16ft fast dinghy	**51**	Lifting position
20	Traversing shaft (over)	**52**	Sinkers
21	Electric winch	**53**	Engine room exhaust vent
22	Chain driving wheels	**54**	Sprocket shaft
23	32ft life cutter (stowed)	**55**	Motor boat engineer's work space
24	25ft fast motor boat (lowering position)	**56**	7-ton electric crane
25	27ft whaler	**57**	Opening (over)
26	25ft fast motor boat (stowed)	**58**	35ft fast seaplane tender
27	Traversing gear hand winch	**59**	Engine room supply vent
28	Reel (over)	**60**	4 carley floats
29	No 2 transmitting mast	**61**	Life belt locker
30	Lifeboat gear locker	**62**	Cordage reel
31	Boat gear store	**63**	Catamaran
32	Shelves (over)	**64**	Balsa raft
		65	Kedge anchor (stored)

J Boats

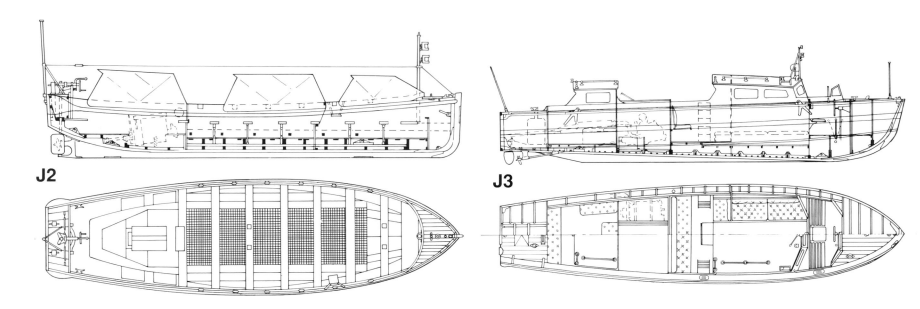

J2 **J3**

J2 36ft **MOTOR PINNACE** (all boat
drawings 1/100 scale)

J3 35ft **FAST MOTOR BOAT**

J4 35ft **FAST SEAPLANE TENDER**

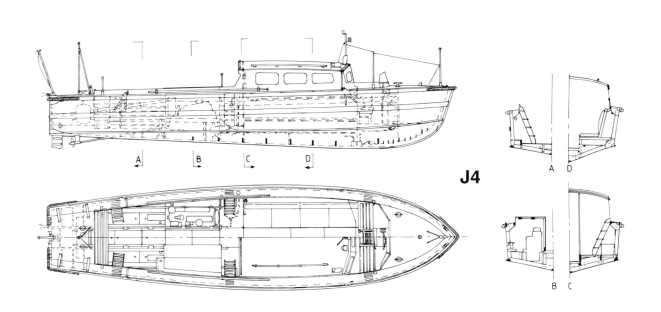

J4

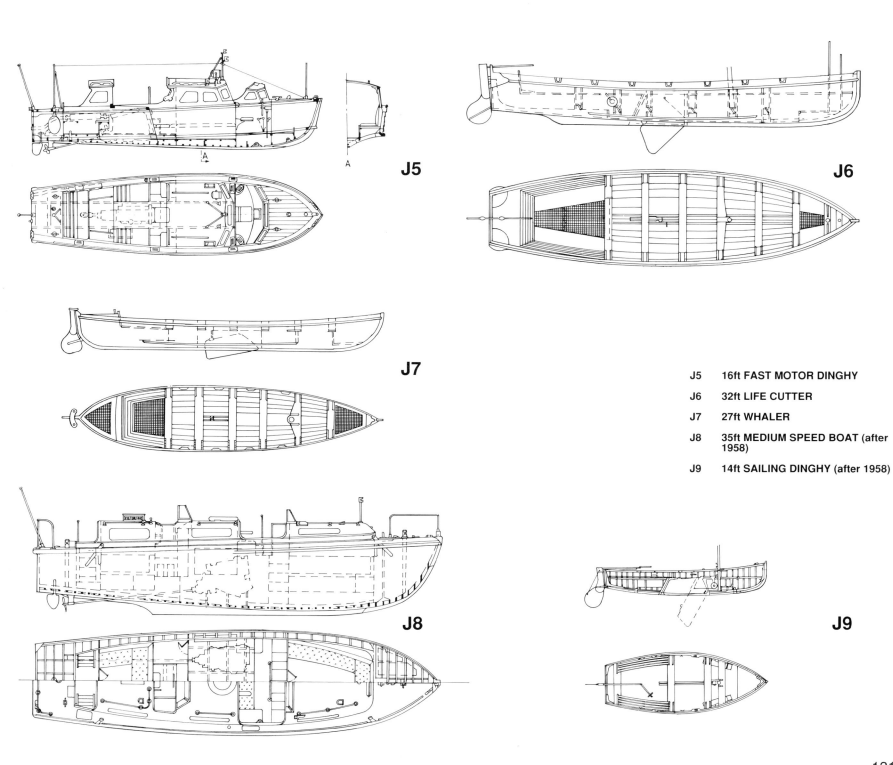

J5

J6

J7

J8

J9

J5   16ft FAST MOTOR DINGHY

J6   32ft LIFE CUTTER

J7   27ft WHALER

J8   35ft MEDIUM SPEED BOAT (after 1958)

J9   14ft SAILING DINGHY (after 1958)

J Boats

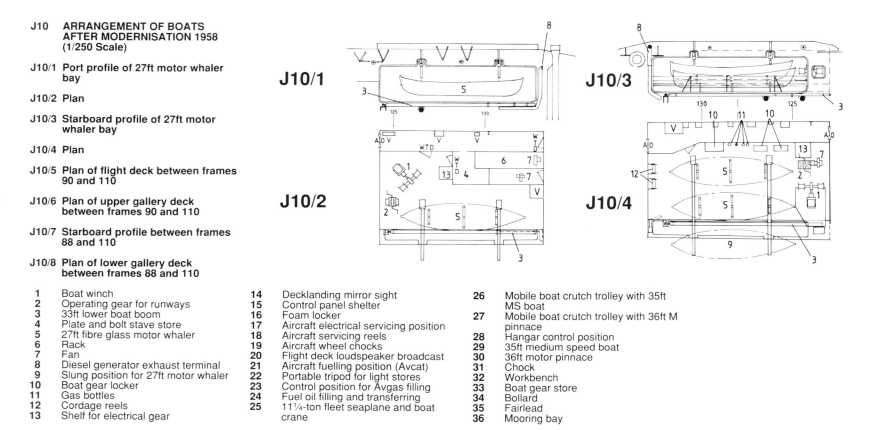

1	Boat winch	14	Decklanding mirror sight	26	Mobile boat crutch trolley with 35ft MS boat
2	Operating gear for runways	15	Control panel shelter	
3	33ft lower boat boom	16	Foam locker	27	Mobile boat crutch trolley with 36ft M pinnace
4	Plate and bolt stave store	17	Aircraft electrical servicing position	
5	27ft fibre glass motor whaler	18	Aircraft servicing reels	28	Hangar control position
6	Rack	19	Aircraft wheel chocks	29	35ft medium speed boat
7	Fan	20	Flight deck loudspeaker broadcast	30	36ft motor pinnace
8	Diesel generator exhaust terminal	21	Aircraft fuelling position (Avcat)	31	Chock
9	Slung position for 27ft motor whaler	22	Portable tripod for light stores	32	Workbench
10	Boat gear locker	23	Control position for Avgas filling	33	Boat gear store
11	Gas bottles	24	Fuel oil filling and transferring	34	Bollard
12	Cordage reels	25	11¼-ton fleet seaplane and boat crane	35	Fairlead
13	Shelf for electrical gear			36	Mooring bay

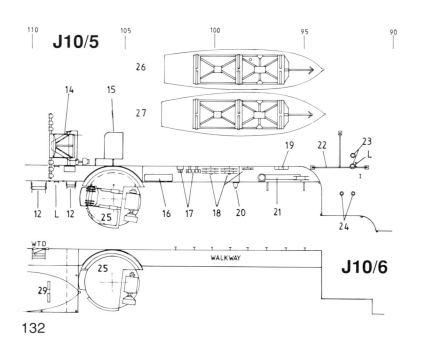

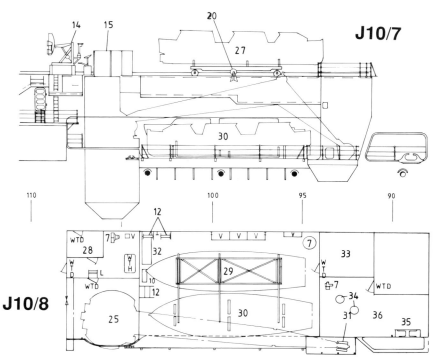

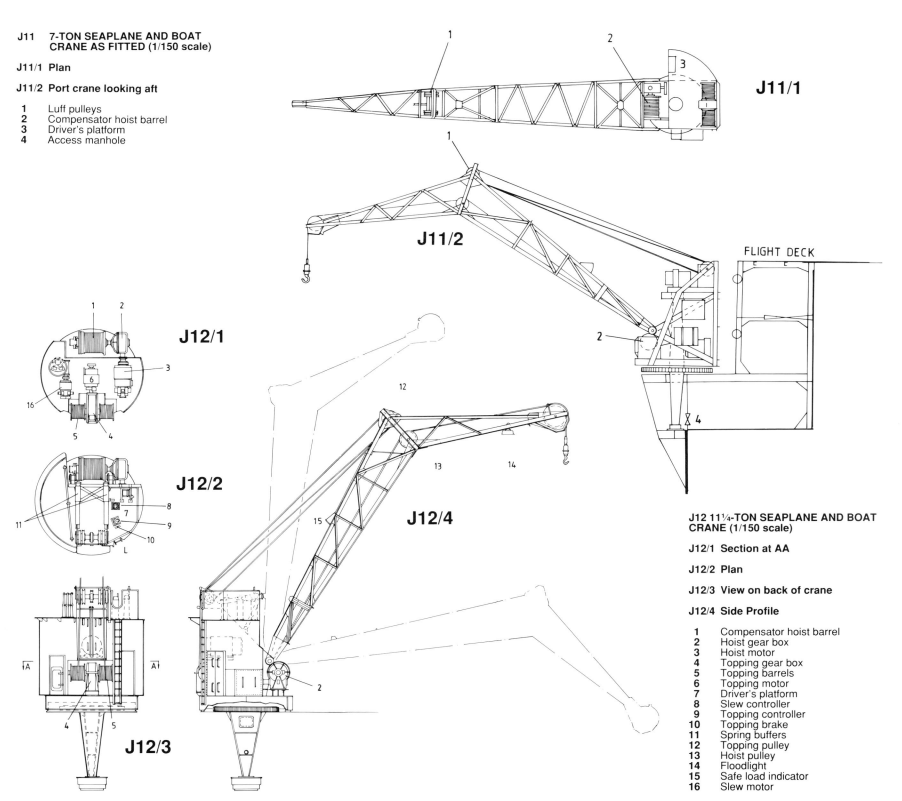

J11 7-TON SEAPLANE AND BOAT CRANE AS FITTED (1/150 scale)

J11/1 Plan

J11/2 Port crane looking aft

1 Luff pulleys
2 Compensator hoist barrel
3 Driver's platform
4 Access manhole

J11/1

J11/2

FLIGHT DECK

J12/1

J12/2

J12/4

J12/3

J12 11¼-TON SEAPLANE AND BOAT CRANE (1/150 scale)

J12/1 Section at AA

J12/2 Plan

J12/3 View on back of crane

J12/4 Side Profile

1   Compensator hoist barrel
2   Hoist gear box
3   Hoist motor
4   Topping gear box
5   Topping barrels
6   Topping motor
7   Driver's platform
8   Slew controller
9   Topping controller
10 Topping brake
11 Spring buffers
12 Topping pulley
13 Hoist pulley
14 Floodlight
15 Safe load indicator
16 Slew motor

133

J Boats

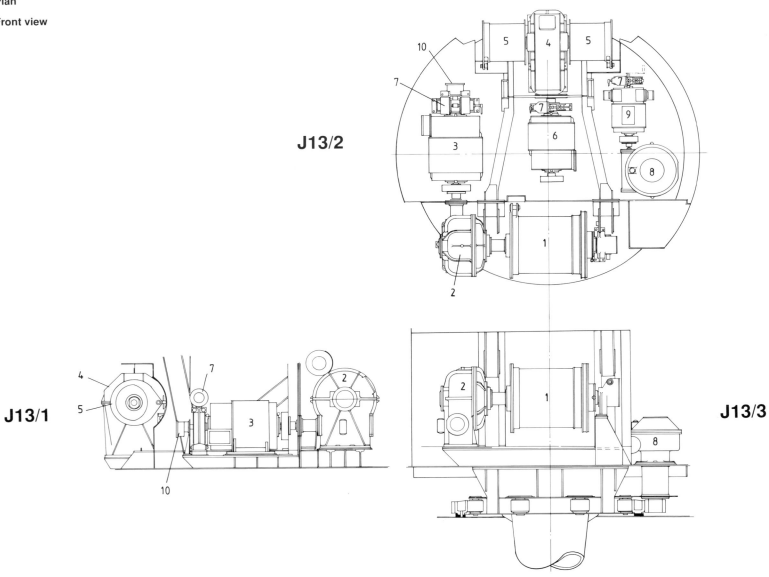

J13/2

J13/1

J13/3

1	Compensator hoist barrel
2	Hoist gear box
3	Hoist motor
4	Topping gear box
5	Topping barrels
6	Luff motor
7	Electrol-mechanical brake
8	Slew gear box
9	Slew motor
10	Over speed trip switch

K Flight deck arrangements

K   **Flight deck arrangements**

K1   **ARRESTER GEAR
ARRANGEMENT AS FITTED**

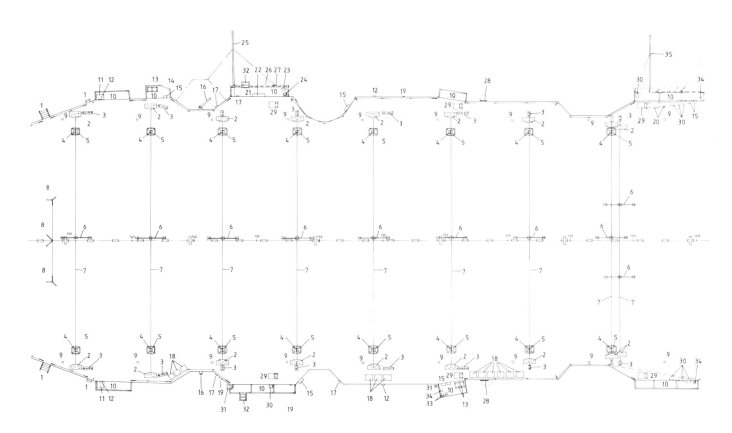

1	Mild steel ladder	**19**	Cleats
2	Sheaves	**20**	Signal flag locker
3	Spray shield	**21**	Arresting gear control platform
4	Swivel	**22**	Control panel
5	Swivel support	**23**	Locker
6	Arrester wire support	**24**	Funnel from engine smith's shop
7	Arrester wire	**25**	No 3 aircraft signalling boom (18ft)
8	Awning and guard stanchions	**26**	Signalling boom stowed
9	Outline light	**27**	Crutch
10	Safety net	**28**	Arm for securing crane
11	Opening with hinged cover	**29**	Pillar light
12	Foot rungs	**30**	Steel helmet bin
13	Pyrene generator	**31**	Galley funnel
14	Firenozzle	**32**	Sector light
15	Hose rack	**33**	Pyrene cylinders
16	Portable davit	**34**	Fire bucket
17	Ladder	**35**	No 2 aircraft signalling boom(18ft)
18	Depth charges		

K2 **CRASH BARRIER**
ARRANGEMENT AS FITTED

K2

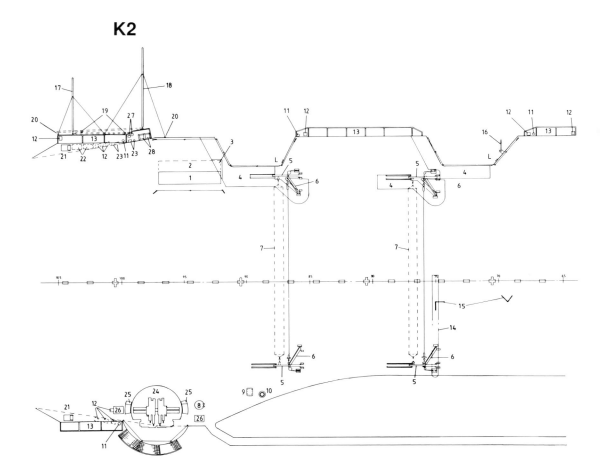

1. Torpedo lift cover
2. Torpedo lift cover in open position
3. Hinged plate in way of lift cover
4. Ramp
5. Stanchion
6. Stay
7. Crash barrier in down position
8. Wireless lead in for RDF mast
9. Ammunition chute
10. RDF aerial mast
11. Fire bucket
12. Steel helmet bin
13. Safety net
14. Conning bridge in operating position
(over)
15. Awning stanchions and stays
16. Spare armature davit
17. No 2 aircraft signalling boom (18ft)
18. No 1 aircraft signalling boom (27ft)
19. Crutch
20. Cleat
21. Pillar light
22. Signal flag locker
23. Hose racks and nozzles
24. 2pdr pom-pom mounting
25. Loading platform
26. Pom-pom ready-use locker
27. Pyrene cylinders
28. Pyrene generator

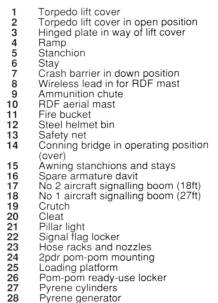

K3

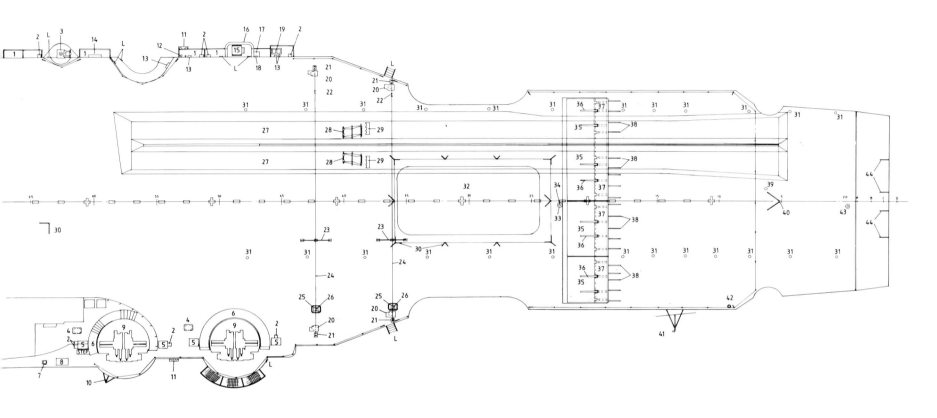

1 Safety net	**17** Opening with hinged cover	**32** Aircraft lift
2 Steel helmet bin	**18** Foot rungs	**33** Watertight scuttle
3 Pom-pom director	**19** Pyrene generator	**34** Hydraulic telescopic mast for second
4 Ammunition chute	**20** Sheave	steaming light
5 Ready-use pom-pom locker	**21** Spray shield	**35** Windscreen
6 Loading platform	**22** Connecting link	**36** Power hinge
7 Sounding machine	**23** Arrester wire support	**37** Drag plate
8 Sounding gear locker	**24** Arrester wire	**38** Rubbing strips for drag plate
9 2pdr pom-pom mounting	**25** Swivel support	**39** Combined steamjet and direction
10 Hinged portable boom	**26** Swivel	light
11 Carrier identification lights	**27** Catapult loading platform	**40** Jackstaff and anchor light
12 Fire bucket	**28** Adjustable guide board	**41** Shaded stem light
13 Hose rack nozzle	**29** Wheel chock	**42** Signal and homing light
14 Control gear	**30** Awning and guard stanchions with	**43** Hand operated telescopic mast
15 Assisted take-off gear control panel	stays	**44** Rails for paint staging
16 Wind deflector	**31** Direction light	

K Flight deck arrangements

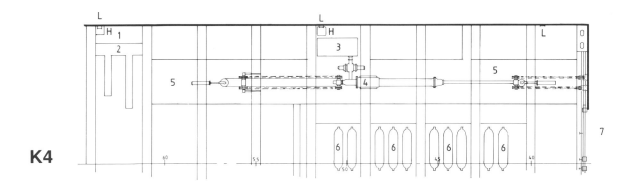

K4

K5/1

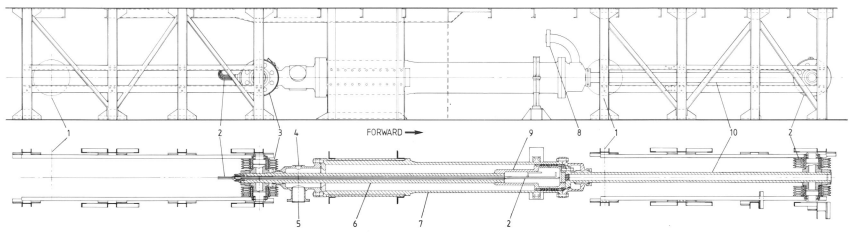

FORWARD →

K5/2

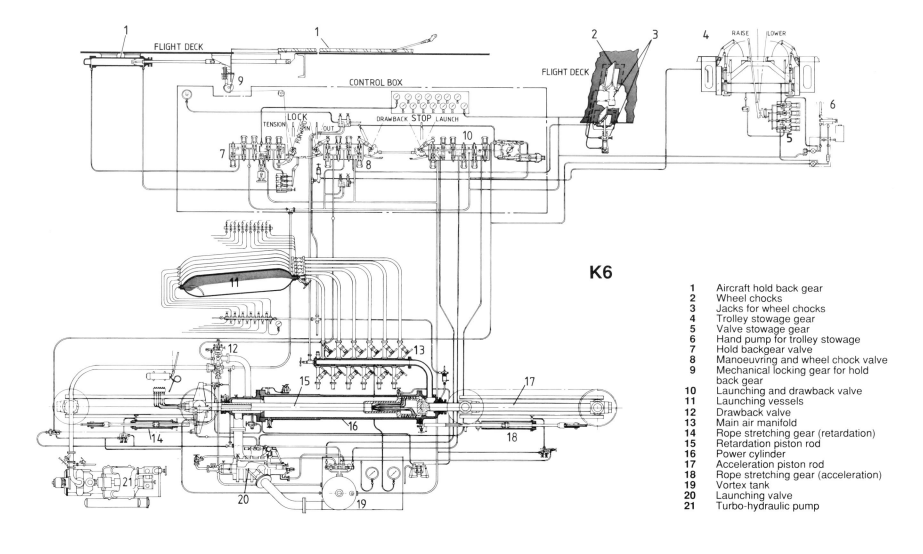

K6

1   Aircraft hold back gear
2   Wheel chocks
3   Jacks for wheel chocks
4   Trolley stowage gear
5   Valve stowage gear
6   Hand pump for trolley stowage
7   Hold backgear valve
8   Manoeuvring and wheel chock valve
9   Mechanical locking gear for hold
     back gear
10   Launching and drawback valve
11   Launching vessels
12   Drawback valve
13   Main air manifold
14   Rope stretching gear (retardation)
15   Retardation piston rod
16   Power cylinder
17   Acceleration piston rod
18   Rope stretching gear (acceleration)
19   Vortex tank
20   Launching valve
21   Turbo-hydraulic pump

K Flight deck arrangements

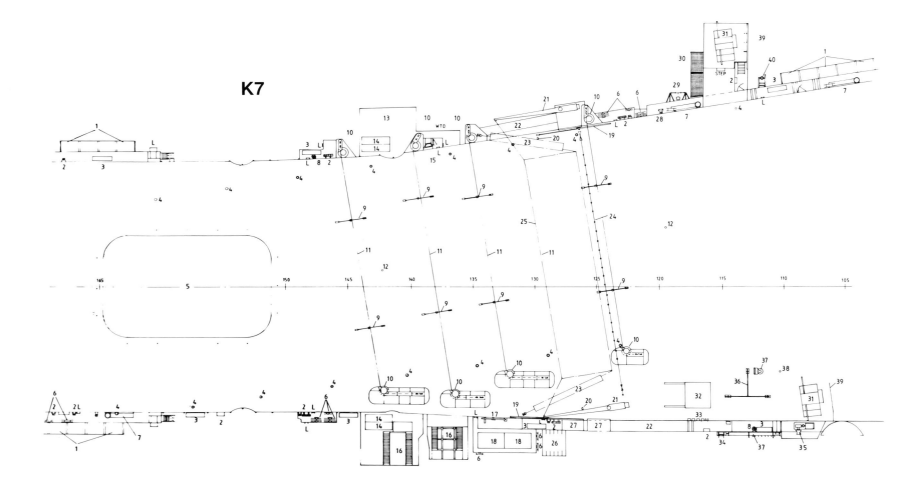

K7

1	Double liferaft and survival stowage	14	Spare barrier net stowage	27	Ready-use barrier net stowage
2	Aircraft engine starter and servicing position	15	Arrester gear and crash barrier control room	28	Hydraulic control valves for whip aerials
3	Foam locker	16	Liquid oxygen tank stowage (LOX)	29	4in aerial trunk
4	Outline light (white)	17	Davit	30	Safety net
5	After aircraft lift	18	Spare barrier pack stowage	31	Deck landing projector sight
6	Reels for engine starter cables	19	Barrier tensioner	32	Weapon lift cover
7	Aircraft fuelling position (Avcat)	20	Pylon bracket	33	Weapon lift switch gear
8	Handwheel operating valves on Avcat filter under	21	Emergency barrier mast in stowed position	34	Cordage reel
		22	Ready-use nylon pack stowage	35	1½-ton electrical winch
9	Arrester wire support	23	Nylon pack undrawn	36	Portable tripod mast
10	Leading sheaves	24	Anchorage wire	37	Stumpmast
11	Arrester wire	25	Outline of barrier net (lowered)	38	Contour light angled deck (red)
12	Centreline lights angled deck (white)	26	Bridge strop stowage	39	Protection screen
13	Buccaneer drop tank stowage			40	Whip aerial

K8

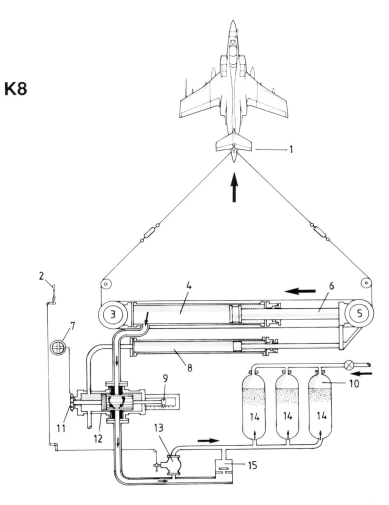

K9

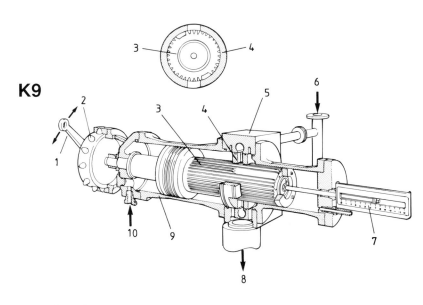

1	Control gear
2	Locking pawls
3	Spline valve
4	Choke ring
5	Centre piece
6	From main cylinder
7	Indicator
8	To air loaded accumulator
9	Receiving cylinder
10	From transmitting cylinder

1	Aircraft hook engaged
2	Flight deck control
3	Fixed cross head
4	Main cylinder
5	Moving cross head
6	Piston rod
7	Control room
8	Transmitting cylinder
9	Indicator
10	Compressed air
11	Control
12	Spline valve
13	Resetting valve
14	Air load accumulators
15	Non-return valve

K Flight deck arrangements

K10/1

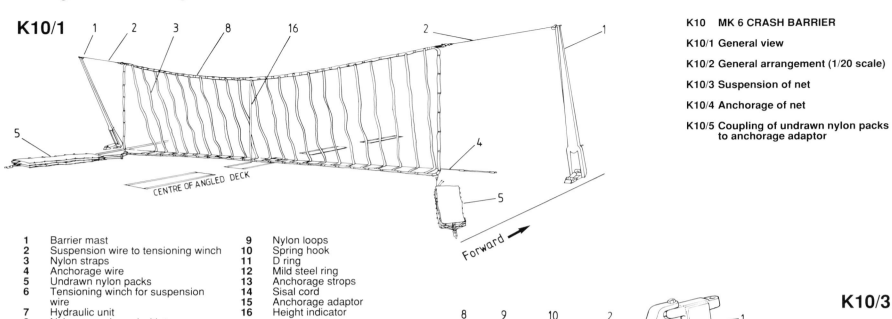

CENTRE OF ANGLED DECK

Forward

1	Barrier mast	9	Nylon loops
2	Suspension wire to tensioning winch	10	Spring hook
3	Nylon straps	11	D ring
4	Anchorage wire	12	Mild steel ring
5	Undrawn nylon packs	13	Anchorage strops
6	Tensioning winch for suspension wire	14	Sisal cord
7	Hydraulic unit	15	Anchorage adaptor
8	Nylon ropes bound with tape	16	Height indicator

K10   MK 6 CRASH BARRIER

K10/1 General view

K10/2 General arrangement (1/20 scale)

K10/3 Suspension of net

K10/4 Anchorage of net

K10/5 Coupling of undrawn nylon packs to anchorage adaptor

K10/2

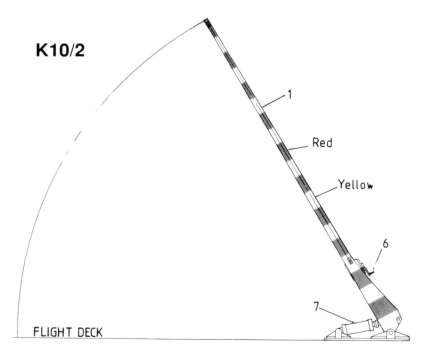

Red

Yellow

FLIGHT DECK

K10/3

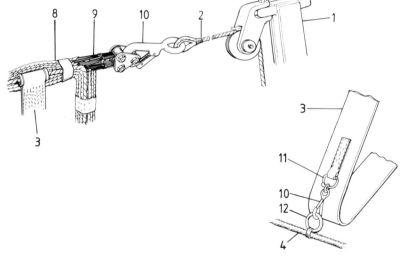

K10/4

K10/5

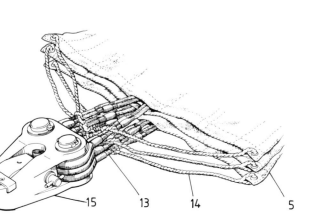

K11 PORT CATAPULT ANCILLIARY LOADING EQUIPMENT (scale)

1 Roller matt short
2 Locking arm to hold chocks in up position for maintenance
3 Sealing strips for auto hold-back loader
4 Catapult shuttle track
5 Hydraulic chock-operating ram
6 Guard plate and guard rails
7 Loading chocks in up position
8 Roller matt long
9 Aircraft loading positioner (ALP)
10 Gearbox
11 Oil drain
12 Reduction unit
13 Servo-operated clutches
14 Hydraulic motor
15 Steam turbines
16 Booster pump
17 Friction clutch
18 Hydraulic drive pump
19 ALP hydraulic drive tank
20 Catapult servo system accumulator
21 To jigger servos
22 Solenoid operated valves
23 To loading chocks
24 Clutch control valve
25 Oil cooler
26 Main hydraulic pump
27 Filter
28 Drain to main oil tank
29 Lub oil supply to ALP
30 Hold-back trough

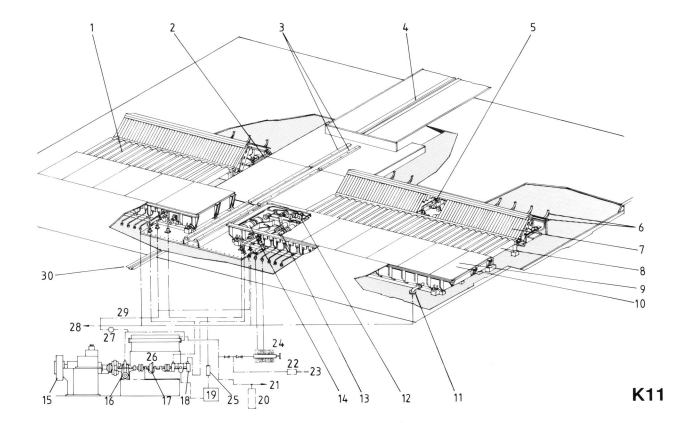

K11

K12

K12 SECTION THROUGH GEARBOX AND ROLLER MATT (1/10 scale)

1 Clutch shaft
2 Cover plates
3 Driven roller
4 Driven shaft

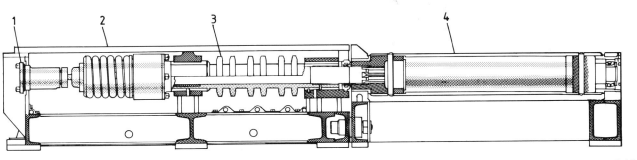

143

K Flight deck arrangements

K13 **SHORTENED VIEW OF STARBOARD BS4 CATAPULT**

1 Port catapult ancilliary loading equipment
2 Cylinder lines
3 Retardation cylinder
4 Hydraulic jigger
5 Operating platform
6 Jigger ropes
7 Exhaust valve
8 Steam receivers
9 Piston group assembly
10 Launching valves
11 Grab
12 Shuttle
13 Deck control position

K13

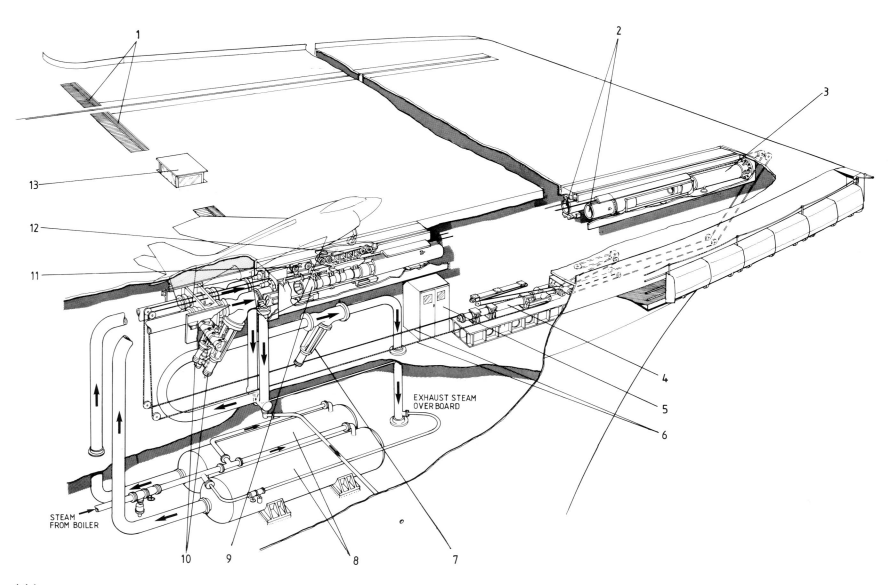

EXHAUST STEAM OVERBOARD

STEAM FROM BOILER

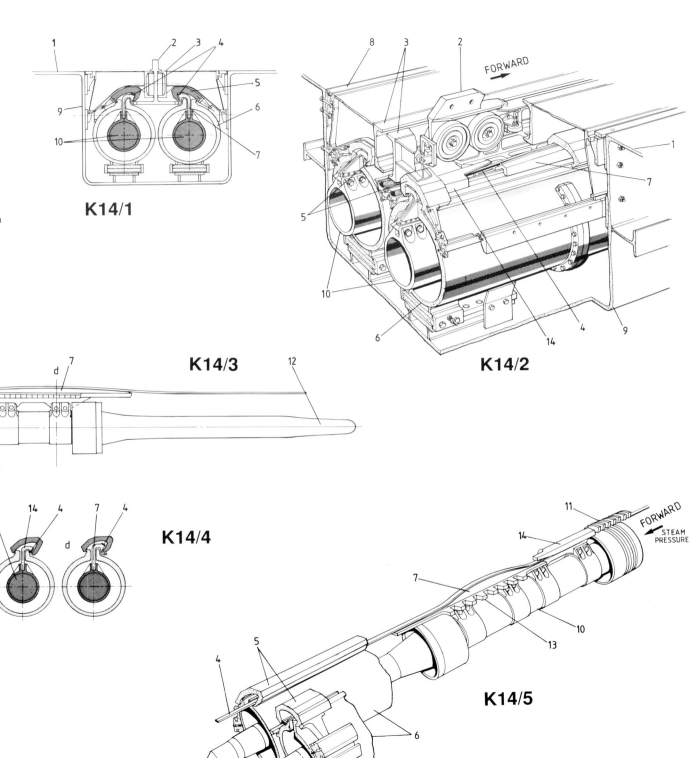

K14 BS4 CATAPULT

K14/1 Cross-section through main cylinders (1/30 scale)

K14/2 Section through cylinder installation

K14/3 Detail of piston assembly and retardation ram (1/30 scale)

K14/4 a Strip seating normally on cylinder and cover
 b Sealing block passing over strip
 c Strip lowered under driving iron
 d Strip raised over driving iron

K14/5 Steam catapult piston

K14/1

K14/2

K14/3

K14/4

K14/5

1	Flight deck
2	Shuttle
3	Tracks
4	Sealing strip
5	Cylinder cover
6	Main cylinder line
7	Driving key
8	Retaining bar
9	Trough
10	Catapult piston
11	Sealing block
12	Retarding ram
13	Driving dogs
14	Driving iron

FORWARD

FORWARD STEAM PRESSURE

145

K Flight deck arrangements

K15 CUTAWAY VIEW OF DECK CONTROL POSITION ON UPPER GALLERY DECK

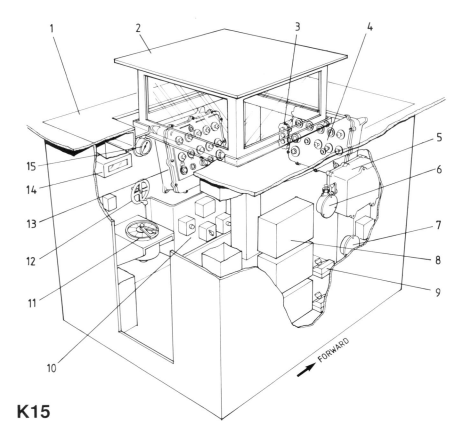

K15

1 Flight deck
2 Retracting canopy
3 Jet baffle buttons
4 Catapult launch box
5 Steam receiver pressure order instrument
6 Steam receiver pressure gauge
7 Pressure gauge for chocks, jet baffle and tail wheel flaps
8 Telephone boxes
9 Telephone plugs
10 Dimmer controls
11 Control order telegraph
12 Aircraft position width setting handwheel
13 Catapult loading box
14 End speed recorder
15 Forward tensioning load control gauge

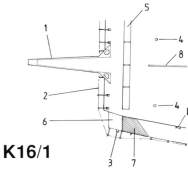

K16/1

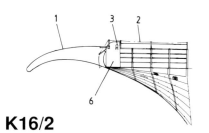

K16/2

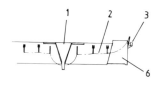

K16/3

K16 BRIDLE CATCHER FITTED OCTOBER 1960 (1/250 scale)

K16/1 Plan of port catapult

K16/2 Port profile

K16/3 Bow view

1 Bridle catcher
2 Magnetic broadcast loop
3 Anchor light
4 Axial deck end light (amber)
5 Bow parked chocks
6 Bridle catchers and control position for parking chocks
7 Galvanised steel grating
8 Port catapult

K17 DIAGRAMATIC DRAWING OF AIRCRAFT FUELLING SYSTEM

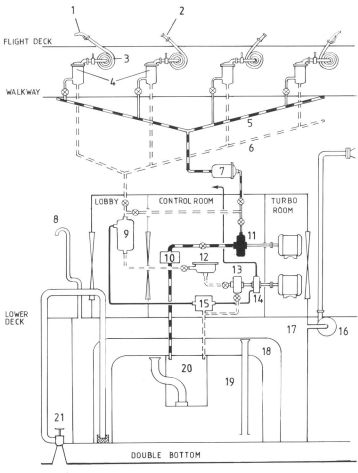

K17

1	Nozzle	**12**	Filter
2	Pressure fuelling nozzle	**13**	Drain pump
3	Hose reel	**14**	Air pump
4	Streamline filters	**15**	Air suction float valve
5	Fuelling system	**16**	Exhaust fan
6	De-fuelling system	**17**	Cofferdam
7	Fram filter	**18**	Saddle tank
8	Natural ventilation inlet	**19**	Main tank
9	Vacuum tank	**20**	Drain off tank
10	Float valve	**21**	Sea valve open
11	Delivery pump		

K18 AVCAT STREAMLINE FILTER

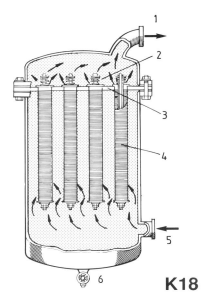

K18

1	Fuel outlet
2	Springs for compressing paper discs
3	Diaphragm plate
4	Paper elements thin paper discs
5	Fuel inlet
6	Drain

K19 DECK LANDING PROJECTOR SIGHT

K19

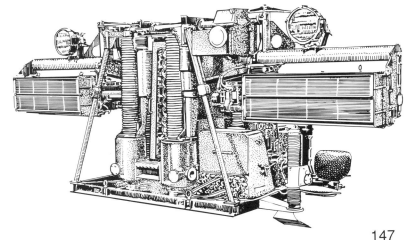

K Flight deck arrangements

K20/1

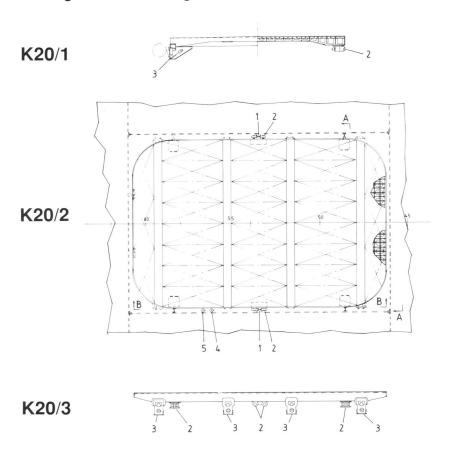

K20/2

K20/3

K20/4

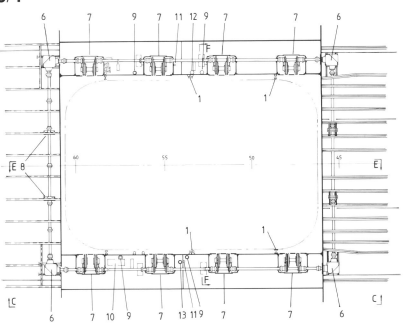

K20/5

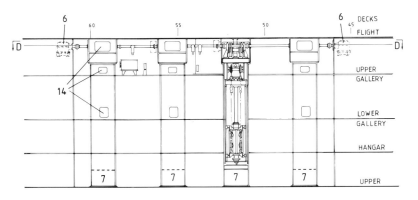

K20/6

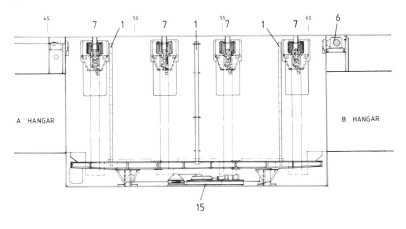

**K20   FORWARD AIRCRAFT LIFT
AFTER MODERNISATION 1958
(1/250 scale)**

K20/1 Part section at BB

K20/2 Plan at flight deck

K20/3 View on AA

K20/4 Section at DD

K20/5 Section at CC

K20/6 Section at EE

K20/7 Section at FF

1	Guide rail
2	Guide rollers
3	Anchorage bracket
4	Emergency stop rod
5	Control rod
6	Corner mitre gear box
7	Jigger trunk
8	Bearing pedestal
9	Solenoid valve for brakes
10	Deck selector
11	Brake pressure switch
12	Keep solenoid valve
13	Keep change-over solenoid valve
14	Access holes
15	Hydraulic unit
16	Platform stops
17	Auxilliary keeps
18	Machinery space
19	Rise and fall platform
20	Air bottle space

**K21   ARRANGEMENT OF FORWARD
AIRCRAFT LIFT MACHINERY
SPACES (1/100 scale)**

K21/1 Plan of upper deck

K21/2 Section at AA

K21/3 Section at BB

K21/4 Section at CC

K21/5 Section at DD

K21/6 Section at EE

K21/7 Section at FF

K21/8 Section at GG

1	Air bottle
2	Pressurised exhaust tank
3	Accumulator
4	'Auto-Klean' strainers
5	Up and down creep solenoid valves
6	Pressure reducing unit
7	Hydro-pneumatic machine
8	Water end
9	Air end
10	By-pass valve solenoid
11	By-pass valve
12	Silencing solenoid
13	Pump
14	Starter
15	Serck oil cooler
16	Roto-plunge ger pump and motor
17	Pump selector
18	Control panel

K21/1

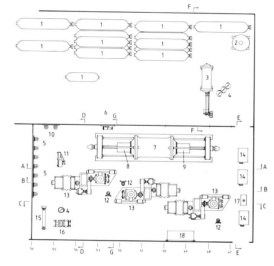

K20/7

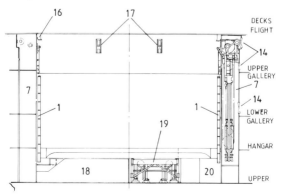

K21/2

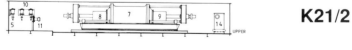

K21/3

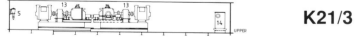

K21/4

K21/5

K21/6

K21/7

K21/8

L Aircraft

K22 JIGGER FOR AIRCRAFT LIFTS
(1/20 scale)

K22/1 End view

K22/2 Side elevation

K22/3 Side elevation

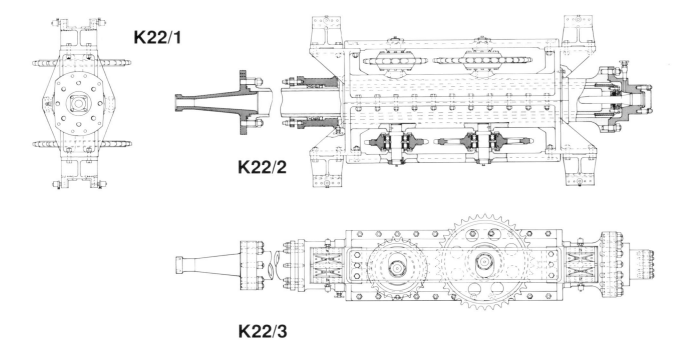

K22/1

K22/2

K22/3

K23 FORWARD BOMB LIFT AFTER
MODERNISATION 1958 (1/50
scale)

K23/1 Section at AA

K23/2 End view

K23/3 Plan

K23/4 Back view

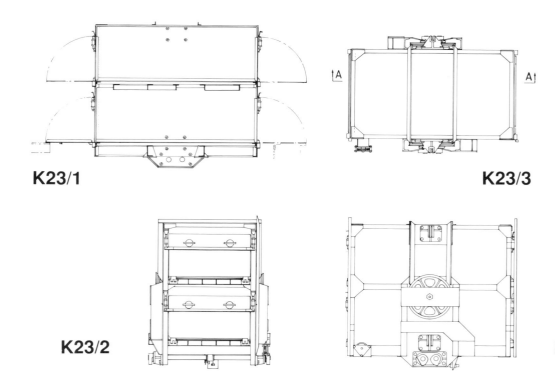

K23/1

K23/3

K23/2

K23/4

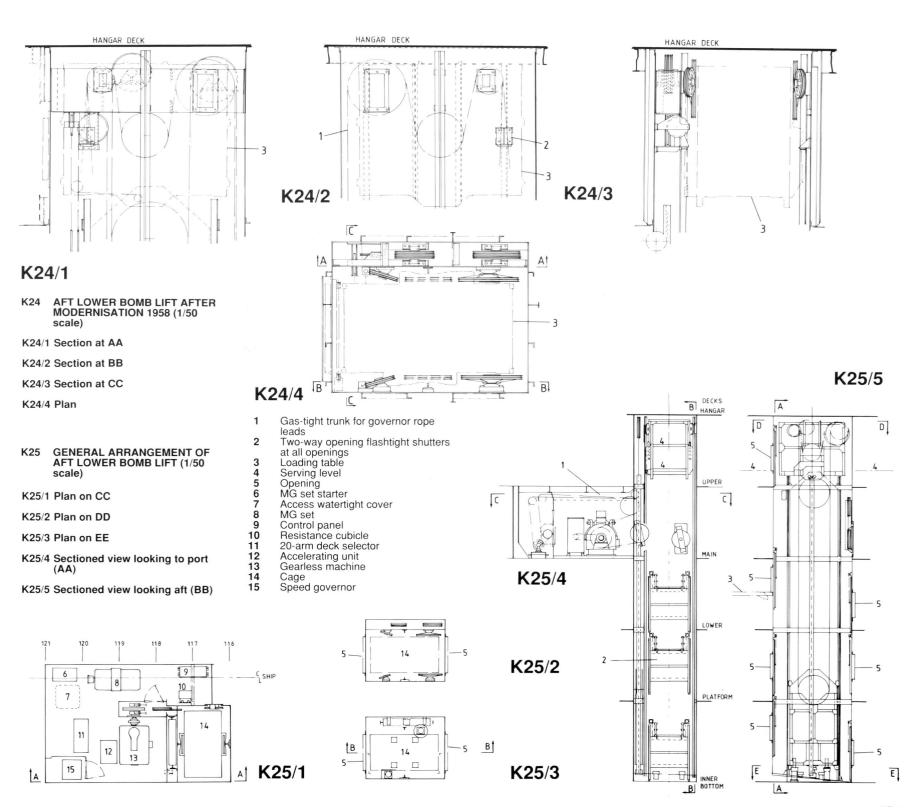

HANGAR DECK

HANGAR DECK

HANGAR DECK

K24/2

K24/3

K24/1

K24 **AFT LOWER BOMB LIFT AFTER MODERNISATION 1958 (1/50 scale)**

K24/1 Section at AA

K24/2 Section at BB

K24/3 Section at CC

K24/4 Plan

K24/4

K25 **GENERAL ARRANGEMENT OF AFT LOWER BOMB LIFT (1/50 scale)**

K25/1 Plan on CC

K25/2 Plan on DD

K25/3 Plan on EE

K25/4 Sectioned view looking to port (AA)

K25/5 Sectioned view looking aft (BB)

1	Gas-tight trunk for governor rope leads
2	Two-way opening flashtight shutters at all openings
3	Loading table
4	Serving level
5	Opening
6	MG set starter
7	Access watertight cover
8	MG set
9	Control panel
10	Resistance cubicle
11	20-arm deck selector
12	Accelerating unit
13	Gearless machine
14	Cage
15	Speed governor

K25/5

K25/4

DECKS

HANGAR

UPPER

MAIN

LOWER

PLATFORM

INNER
BOTTOM

K25/1

K25/2

K25/3

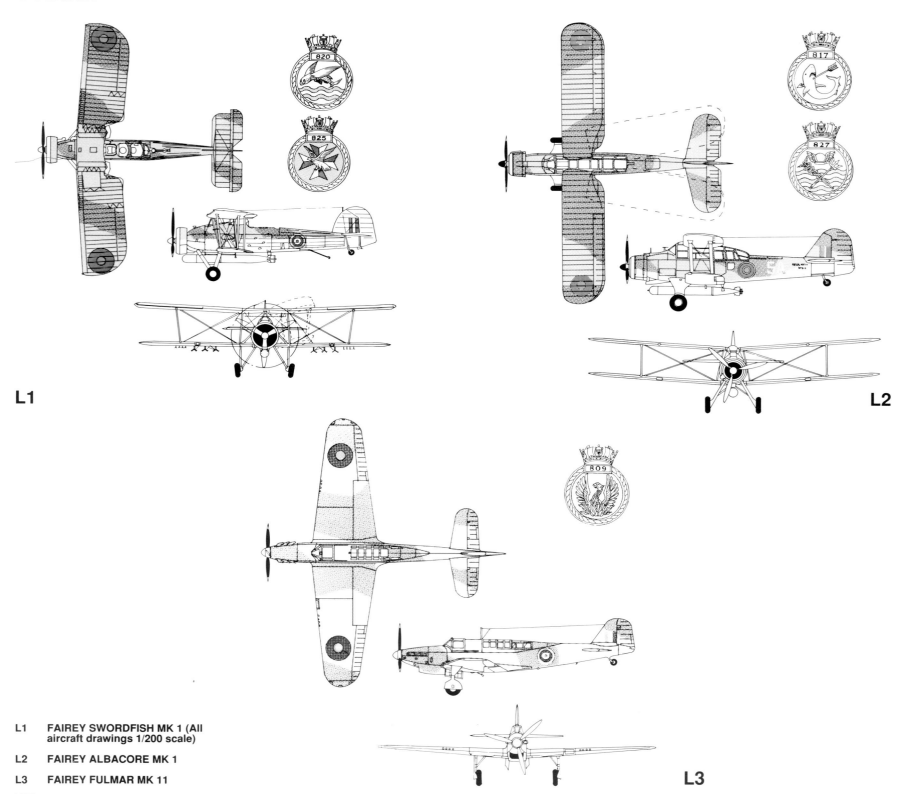

L1

L2

L3

L1   **FAIREY SWORDFISH MK 1 (All aircraft drawings 1/200 scale)**

L2   **FAIREY ALBACORE MK 1**

L3   **FAIREY FULMAR MK 11**

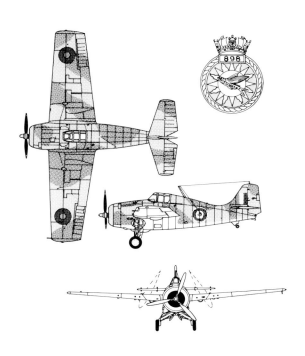

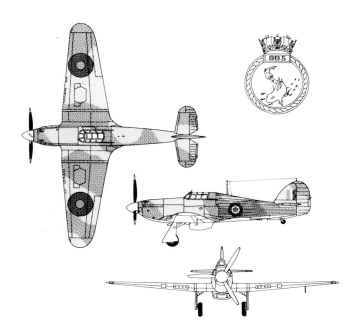

L4

L5

L6

L4   **GRUMMAN MARTLET MK IV**

L5   **HAWKER SEA HURRICANE MK 1B**

L6   **SUPERMARINE SEAFIRE MK IIC**

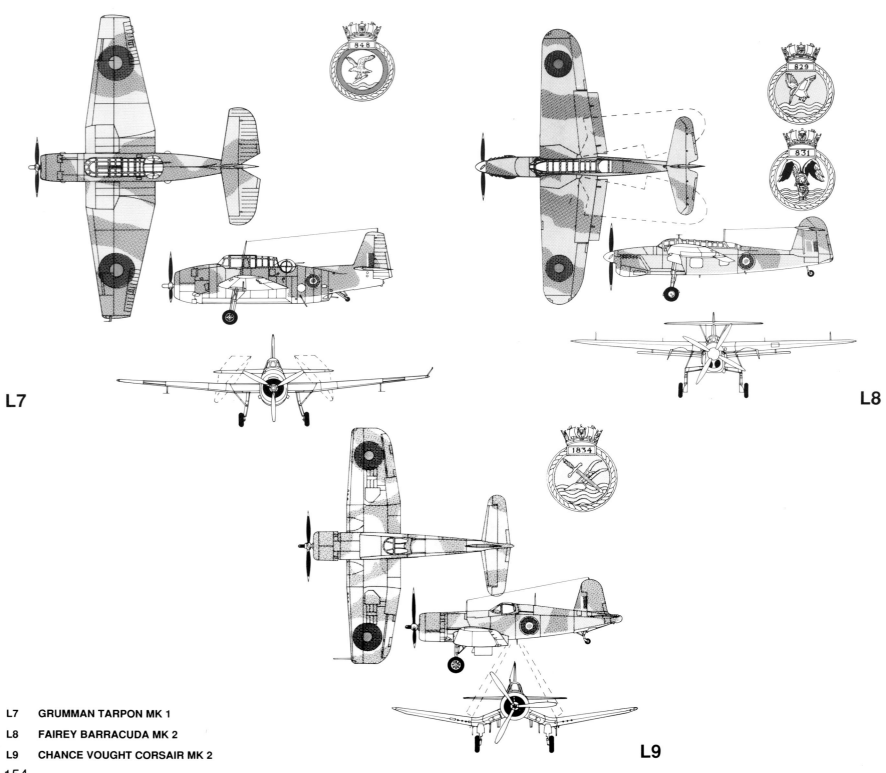

L7   **GRUMMAN TARPON MK 1**

L8   **FAIREY BARRACUDA MK 2**

L9   **CHANCE VOUGHT CORSAIR MK 2**

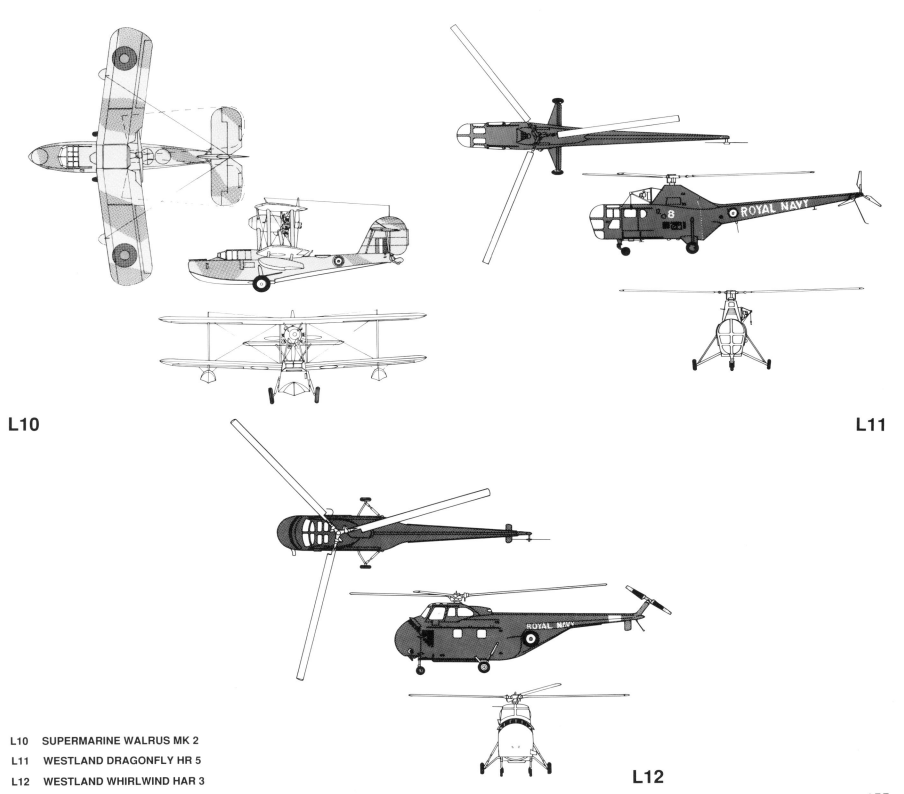

L10

L11

L12

L10   SUPERMARINE WALRUS MK 2

L11   WESTLAND DRAGONFLY HR 5

L12   WESTLAND WHIRLWIND HAR 3

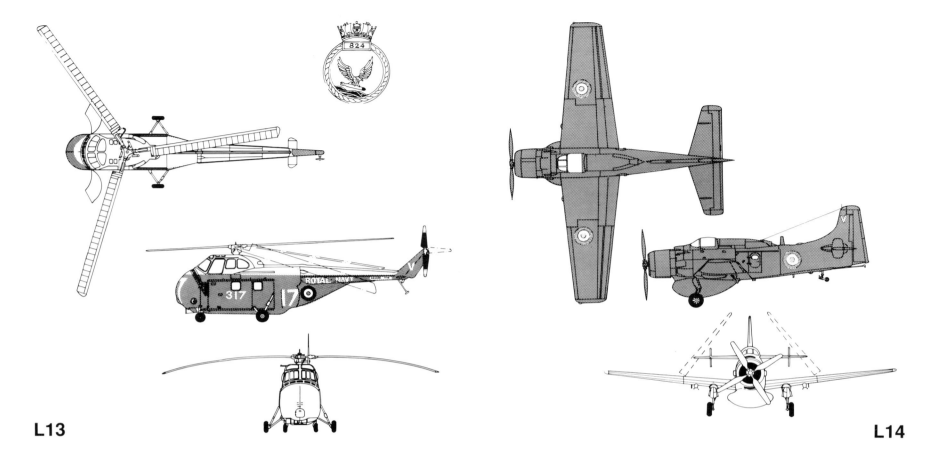

L13

L14

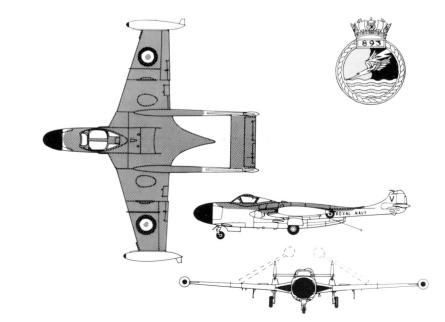

L15

L13   WESTLAND WHIRLWIND HAS 7

L14   DOUGLAS SKYRAIDER AEW 1

L15   DE HAVILLAND SEA VENOM FAW
       21

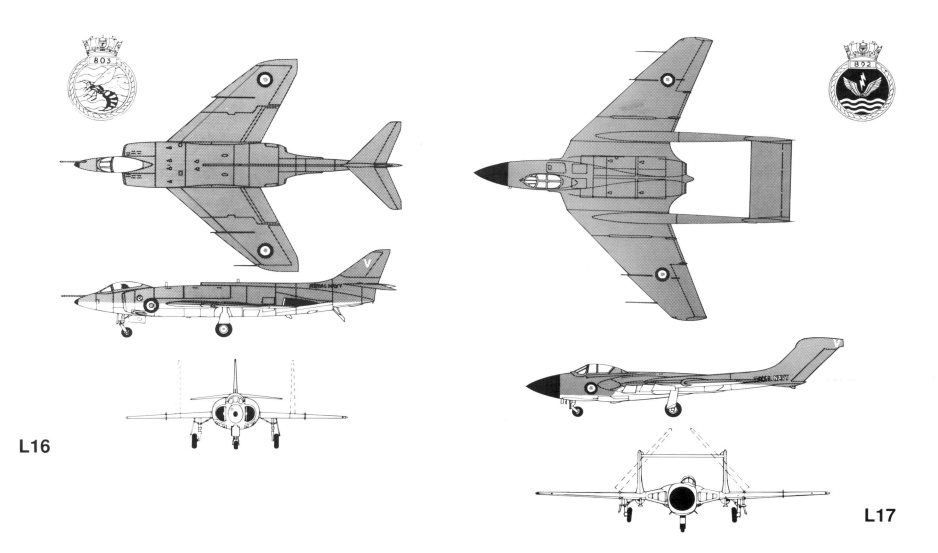

L16

L17

L16   SUPERMARINE SCIMITAR

L17   DE HAVILLAND SEA VIXEN FAW 1

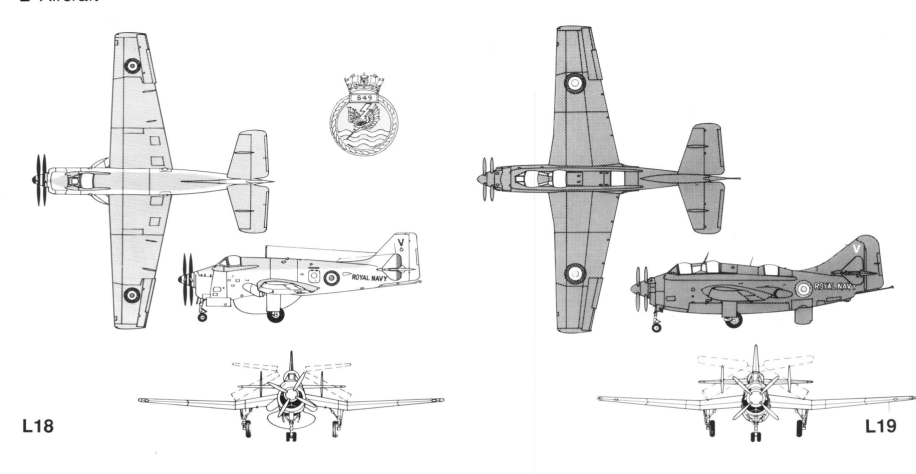

L18

L19

L18   FAIREY GANNET AEW 3

L19   FAIREY GANNET COD 4

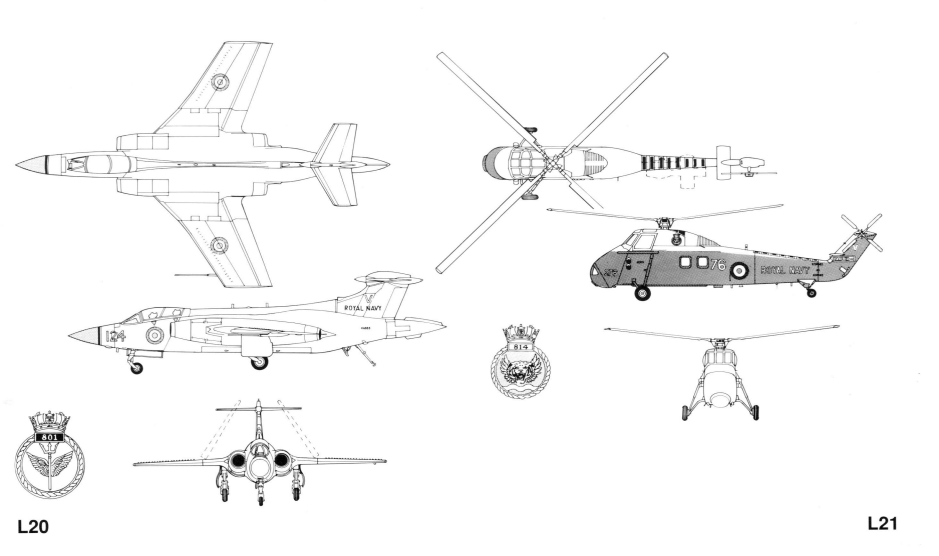

L20

L21

L20   BLACKBURN BUCCANEER S1

L21   WESTLAND WESSEX HAS 1

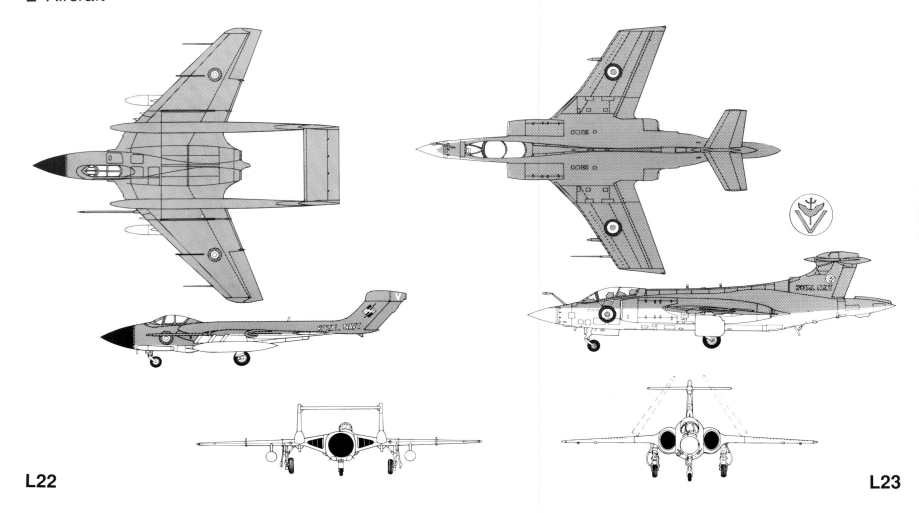

L22

L23

**L22   HAWKER SIDDELEY SEA VIXEN
        FAW 2**

L23   BLACKBURN BUCCANEER S 2